RESEARCH METHODS

How to design and conduct a successful project

Peter Marshall

How To Books

Cartoons by Mike Flanagan

British Library Cataloguing in Publication Data

A catalogue record for this book is available from the British Library.

First published in 1997 by How To Books Ltd, Plymbridge House,
Estover Road, Plymouth PL6 7PZ, United Kingdom. Tel: (01752) 202301.
Fax: (01752) 202331.

Note: The material contained in this book is set out in good faith for general guidance and no liability can be accepted for loss or expense incurred as a result of relying in particular circumstances on statements made in this book. The laws and regulations may be complex and liable to change, and readers should check the current position with the relevant authorities before making personal arrangements.

Produced for How To Books by Deer Park Productions.
Typeset by Concept Communications (Design & Print) Ltd, Crayford, Kent.
Printed and bound by Cromwell Press, Broughton Gifford, Melksham, Wiltshire

Contents

List of illustrations

Preface

Research is not simply describing what you find; it goes further than that. When we speak of research we mean studying something at a deeper level so that we can explain it and predict its behaviour. For some researchers the goal is to understand the world views and ways of life of others, but this still involves more than mere description. They are not simply painting a picture of what they see, they are delving below the surface so that they can make sense of it.

Textbooks on research methods often take a rather 'all or nothing' approach. They tend to be highly comprehensive and technical and rarely very user-friendly. Not everyone has the need to plough through fine detail that does not directly apply to their task in hand. Many people who devote part of their time to research projects are leading busy lives besides, either studying other areas or carrying out other duties. They need to be able to find the information they are looking for quickly and in plain, concise English. This book aims to satisfy such requirements.

Effort has been made to avoid sexism in the language in this book. This is not always easy to do, since constructions like 'he or she', 'he/she', 'him or her' and 'him/her' increase the length of sentences and the complexity of the language. This, in turn, makes the text more difficult to read. To achieve the desired effect, pronouns used for 'researchers', 'investigators' and other subjects have been the neutral ones, like 'they' and 'them', even though the subject may have been singular. As far as possible, such subjects have been referred to in the plural form anyway. Where a male pronoun has had to be used it should be taken as standing for both males and females.

Peter Marshall

1
Choosing the Questions to Ask

The number of questions we can ask about the world around us is infinite. How can we decide where to start? How can we decide what is a useful question? Poncaire provided us with a set of rules for this.

FOCUSING ON THE MOST GENERAL FACTS

Those facts which will provide an answer to the greatest number of questions are, initially, the most useful.

In the early years of educational research some social scientists devoted their attention and resources to finding evidence of a relationship between achievement and social class. This information was of greater value than would have been a discovery that achievement was related to parents' attitudes to education. There were, and still are, many factors besides attitudes to education which serve to disadvantage working class children and advantage middle class ones. Negative attitudes to education at home may not have explained some working class children's underachievement, for their parents may have valued education highly. Other facts, like attitudes of neighbouring children towards school and lack of money to buy books, may have caused them to underachieve instead. All these situations were more likely to be found in the homes of manual workers than in those of white-collar and professional ones.

By confirming a statistical association at this more general conceptual level a relatively large proportion of underachievement could be explained. Much less of the problem could have been accounted for if attention had been focused, instead, upon particular factors such as 'parental or neighbourhood attitudes towards education', or 'poverty in the home'.

- The more questions a fact can answer – that is, the more scope it has – the more useful it is to science and society.

Beginning with facts of wide scope

Facts of considerable scope provide relatively important pieces of the jigsaw puzzle, for they serve as a guide for the attentions of subsequent researchers. The discovery that socio-economic group is an important influence on school achievement, for instance, provided researchers with the opportunity to take the concept of socio-economic group to bits. They could then set about examining all the things which distinguish one group from another in educationally relevant ways.

In this way more precise knowledge of how socio-economic group affects achievement became known. These more particular factors we call **process variables**, while the concept of socio-economic group is termed a **frame variable**.

FOCUSING ON THE LARGE AND THE SMALL SCALE

There's an art to doing jigsaw puzzles. We don't just take any bit and try to place it in its appropriate space. We would never get anywhere doing that. We start with the outer rim or with meaningful bits of central features – an eye, followed by a matching eye, and then a nose.

Beginning with induction

Scientific knowledge is a jigsaw puzzle too, so we need to build up the picture in a similar way if we are going to make progress efficiently. When an area of inquiry is in its infancy there are no scientific theories from which to hypothesise. Research can only begin by **induction**. The bits need to be put together by whatever clues are available (see page 17), just as those who do jigsaw puzzles rely on the straight edges for building up the outer rim, and their familiarity with faces, houses, cars and other familiar objects to construct the inner features.

Developing hypotheses and theories

Once the outer rim and the central features are complete, though, calculated guesses can be made about what details connect the two. These suggest what kinds of pieces we should look for to fill in the middle-ground. Things work in the same way in the scientific picture. The last pieces we tend to put in are those which link the large scale to the small scale pictures; we do it by making calculated guesses (**hypotheses**) and testing them with data, to build **theories**.

SEEKING THE FACTS WHICH MAKE MOST SENSE OF THE PICTURE

When working on either the cental features, or the periphery of a jigsaw we look for the bits which make most sense of the picture.

Think about it. If you have built up part of a tall-masted ship and a part of a sunset, a piece that contains a bit of both will move the picture on no end, for it will fix the position of one of the sections you have built up in relation to the other. This would be far more productive than gathering together pieces to build quite a different section from scratch.

The same applies to building the scientific jigsaw puzzle. Look for the facts which give harmonious order to the picture already there, rather than isolated facts which will, perhaps, just add to the confusion.

The value of extreme cases

Rare and extreme cases are always worth studying if they have not already been well tested. This is because they can reveal the limitations of the knowledge to date. They can tell us whether there are exceptions which a theory does not explain and whether a theory holds true for the full range of independent variable measurements. IQ, for example, is a good predictor of school success over most of the range, but it does not work so well beyond a certain level.

If limits are found to a theory's scope, other theories can be worked on to explain that range of phenomena the current theory does not provide for.

SUMMARY

- Look for general facts.
- Focus on the large or the small scale.
- It can be useful to study rare or extreme cases.
- Facts which contribute to a harmonious ordering of knowledge are worth seeking.

QUESTIONS AND ANSWERS

1. *Isn't there a case for avoiding the guidelines and just fishing for whatever you find – going out to explore without preconceptions?*

   Trawling in the fact pool represents an inefficient use of resources. You are likely to end up with isolated facts. In contrast, if you strategically direct your search the outcome could be not only a discovery of new facts but also a piecing together of facts which are already known. This way, in addition to the individual facts a higher order knowledge emerges. Searching without definite purpose is like picking up jigsaw pieces and wondering where they go. Searching with a purpose, on the other hand, is like hunting for a jigsaw piece which will link together sections already made.

2. *Surely a significant factor in the choice of what to research is whether you can obtain funding for it?*

   The projects which set out to study facts which funding bodies consider the most useful are the ones which are most likely to receive their financial support.

CASE STUDIES

George focuses on the large scale

George's research focuses on the large scale. He takes his data from a random sample of a **working universe** which is, itself, a representative sample of the general population. His working universe is the sample members of the Child Health and Education Survey. This is an ongoing (longitudinal) study collecting comprehensive data on everyone born in the UK during one particular week in 1972.

George does not consciously look out for extreme cases, although he is always interested in them and accepts their value. He is well aware that they are what mark out the boundaries between one category of attributes and another.

Sylvia focuses on the small scale

Sylvia seeks to describe the outlooks of victims of violence. She is particularly interested in finding common threads in the different kinds of violence she hears about. These may be useful in training counsellors and social workers, and in the development of social policy where it refers to this area.

Sylvia's studies are all focused on the small scale: women's refuges and victims of isolated cases of violence reported in the newspapers.

Her goal is understanding rather than explaining or predicting, so the methodological requirements of the more empiricist science – randomisation, control, etc – are unnecessary. The knowledge Sylvia is seeking to log will always be inseparable from the situational and personal aspects of the victims. Some degree of generalisation to the general population can be achieved by making allowances for these local and personal influences.

Sylvia is interested in the common experiences of violence, but also the extreme and the unusual ones. The former help to define the parameters of her research and indicate whether this social problem is getting worse. The latter may provide knowledge of the direction this social problem is taking. It may indicate whether new forms of violence, or new emotional responses to it, are beginning to appear and whether the level of help and support available is changing.

Graham studies extreme cases

Graham is part of a research team studying memory. Currently favoured memory theory is not entirely satisfactory in explaining the data. There are inconsistencies. Some of the answers, the team thinks, might be found by studying extreme or rare cases of memory quality.

Where extreme cases are concerned, large-scale data is accessible. To produce generalisable findings it is appropriate to focus on this scale. The rare cases, however, by their very nature, will never be available in the large scale.

DISCUSSION POINTS

1. Consider an area of knowledge in which you would like to carry out research.

2. Can you think of any extreme or rare cases which may usefully be studied? How might studying them serve to advance knowledge?

3. Try to think of two examples of research which have focused on the large scale and the small scale respectively. On what grounds have you categorised them as large and small scale?

4. Is there any justification for 'trawling in the fact pool' to see what you can find, as opposed to not going searching before you know what you are looking for?

2
Getting to Grips with Theory

UNDERSTANDING THEORY

The scientific meaning

In the scientific sense a theory is two or more interrelated hypotheses that have been supported by evidence. This is different from the more commonly used meanings of the term, to refer to the written work side of a craft course in a training college or one of Inspector Morse's hunches.

Theory is not a 'law'

A theory is also different from a law, for a theory explains or can predict something in a proportion of cases, but a law explains something in *every* case. Many laws have been discovered to explain phenomena in the physical sciences, but they are not common in the social sciences.

An example of a law in the social sciences is the law of diminishing returns. This tells us that increasing applications of a factor of production (*eg* land, labour, or capital) in an enterprise will provide increasing returns only up to a point. After this the reverse will begin to happen unless the other factors are increased to bring things back into balance.

Strong and weak theories

Theories can be categorised as strong or weak.

- Strong theories many be used for prediction.
- Weak theories are only sufficient for explanation.

The strongest theories will be expressed in quantitative, rather than qualitative, terms.

Working within paradigms

All scientists work within **paradigms**. Paradigms are particular ways of thinking about their subject matter which they share with others of like mind. They include:

- assumptions
- conceptualisations
- values
- attitudes
- orientations
- beliefs.

Different paradigms have their own preferred methods and theories. Psychologists who have grown up, so to speak, in what is known as the behaviourist paradigm would not consider it necessary to understand a patient's experience of a neurotic illness. They would, instead, focus on the behaviour. Appropriate therapy would be by means of behaviour modification techniques. In contrast, psycholoanalysts would want to explore the patient's history to find the cause. They would expect to find it in some repressed conflict and they would seek to cure the condition by bringing this to the patient's conscious awareness.

Paradigms have advantages and disadvantages.

- An advantage is that they prevent scientists wasting time on problems they are not best equipped to solve. In this way they facilitate the benefits of specialisation.
- A disadvantage is that they blinker researchers to other valid ways of looking at the issues.

STARTING WITH FACTS OR THEORIES

The development of scientific knowledge can progress by focusing initially on facts or theories. These methods are referred to as **induction** and **deduction** respectively.

When researchers first begin to open up any new line of enquiry there will be no useful theories available from which to deduce propositions for testing. Knowledge has to begin with collecting facts and then trying to find some order in them. This is known as induction.

It would be naive to say that no theory at all is present at this stage. As human beings we could not make sense of anything without theory, however crude, or even erroneous, it may be. What is meant by lack of theory here is lack of 'scientific theory'.

Deduction is the technique by which knowledge develops in more mature fields of enquiry. It involves a sort of logical leap, going a stage further than the theory provides. Data is then collected to test it.

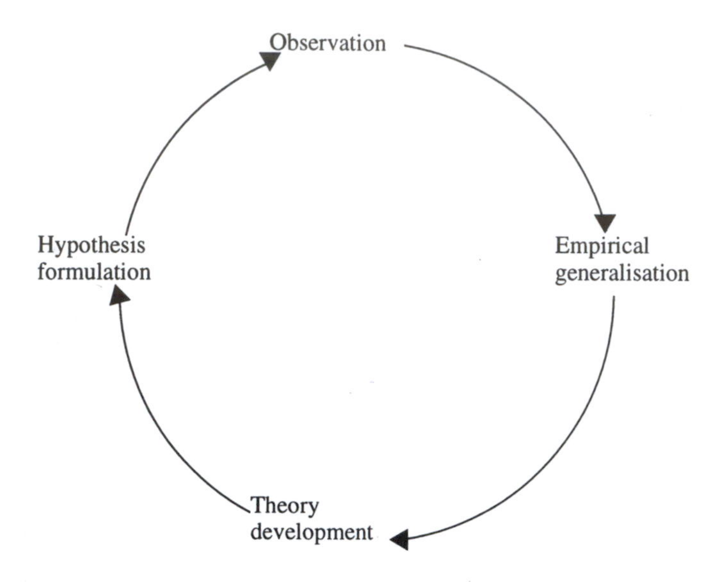

Fig. 1. The circular process of science.

PROGRESSIVE FOCUSING

If you are interested in doing research in a particular field the way to start is to familiarise yourself with the general knowledge in that area. Collect everything you can from any source you can to build a file. Select a more precise sub-area that you find most interesting and study that area in great depth. Analyse your notes to impose an order that is meaningful to you.

BUILDING THEORY

Using concepts

Physical scientists study real, tangible things: atoms, molecules, planetary systems and so on. Social scientists study something much more abstract: behaviour, human ability, relationships between people and things like this. These things are not real in the physical sense; they are intangible, existing only in the mind. These are **concepts**.

Quantifiable and non-quantifiable concepts

Some concepts are of a quantifiable nature and others are not. IQ, for example, is a concept that refers to the level of a person's educational potential and it is easily measurable. The concept of social class, on the other hand, is not. We cannot impute an exact measurement of the social distance between professional, managerial, unskilled white-collar, skilled manual and unskilled manual workers.

Using models

A **model** is a conceptualisation of the way two or more concepts relate to each other. An explanatory model provides an explanation of the mechanisms that underlie such relationships.

Models can be expressed verbally or diagrammatically. If they are expressed diagrammatically there are conventions as to how they should be drawn. For example, concepts are usually represented as circles, and lines of influence are represented by double lines, single lines or broken lines depending on whether the influence is strong, moderate or weak. An example is Plowden's model of influences on educational attainment.

Linear and non-linear models

Models are not always this complex. Sometimes a model may simply amount to a statement that two concepts are linearly related. This is known as a **linear model** and may be expressed as a graph.

The relationship may not always be linear, of course. Thomas Malthus's model of population growth provided that levels of food resources increase arithmetically while population levels increase geometrically. Consequently, population levels would always outstrip food resource levels unless birth control or natural disasters checked the growth of population levels.

Formulating hypotheses

When scientists wish to find out whether two things are related they formulate a statement that they are. This is called a **hypothesis**. It is conventional for scientists to state two hypotheses: hypotheses 1 (H_1) and what is called a **null hypothesis** (H_0). The null hypothesis simply states that the expected relationship will *not* be found.

There is a good reason for this. Science can never prove things; it can only disprove them. If evidence supports a proposition, it is only the best evidence *so far*. Other evidence may be uncovered in the future which will tell quite a different story. So scientists set out to do what they are able to do – disprove something. The nearest they can expect to get to proving their target hypothesis is to disprove its null hypothesis, *ie* the one which says that the relationship they suspect exists does not do so.

Constructs

A **theoretical construct** is a statement, supported by evidence, that two concepts are related in some way. Do not confuse this with a theory; that requires two or more interrelated constructs.

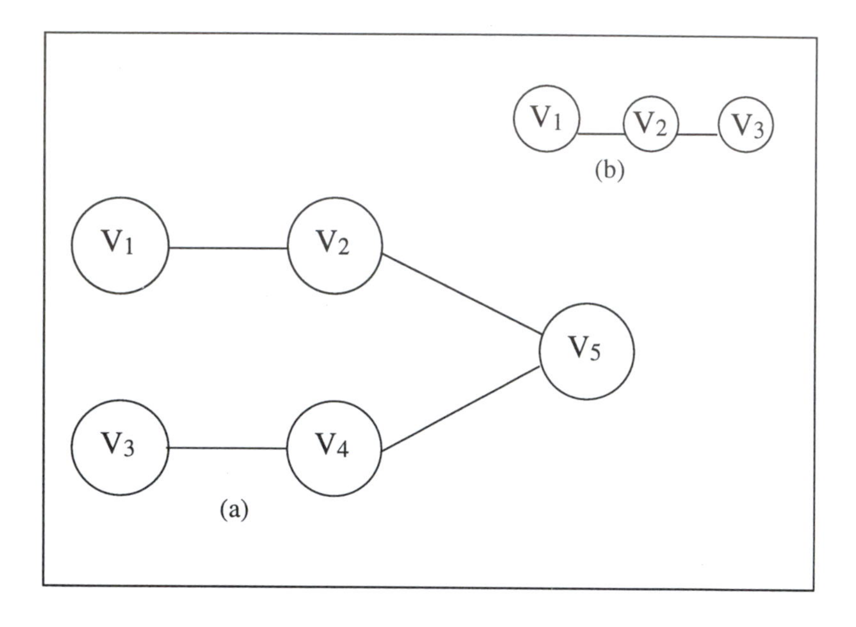

Fig. 2. Simple examples of variable relationships which contain the minimum requirements for theories.

Understanding variables

A **variable** is a concept which can differ in its essence. The sex of a person is a variable, since it can take one of two forms, male or female. The content of some variables tends to differ in measurable degrees, so we call them **quantitative variables**. Age is one example.

Working with scales

Scales are ways in which concepts can differ. Types of scale used in scientific enquiry are as follows.

- nominal
- ordinal
- interval
- ratio.

If a variable is measurable only on a **nominal** scale it means it is completely non-quantitative. An example of this kind of scalar property of a variable is religion. A person's religion can fall into any of the categories of Catholic, Protestant, Muslim, Jew, *etc*. It would be unscientific to attempt to rank these in any order of importance, or award them any quantified values.

If a variable has **ordinal** scalar properties it means the data can be ranked, although no precise calibration can be applied, *ie* the differences between the ranks cannot be quantified. Differences in people's power and authority, as represented on a company structure chart, take this form.

If a variable has **interval** scalar properties it means the differences between the rankings can be quantified, but there is no absolute zero point. IQ is one such variable.

If a variable is said to have **ratio** scalar properties then not only are the calibrations between the rankings precisely quantifiable, but the scale also has an absolute zero point. Temperature is one such variable.

Using language with care

The language used in theory construction should be precise and unambiguous. All concepts and the relationships between them should be clearly defined. Although this is not always feasible, mathematical language (algebraic equation) is preferable.

Explaining and predicting

Scientific theories seek to explain or predict things.

For a theory to be able to predict something adequately it needs to be much stronger in its explanatory power than if it is to be used merely for explaining something that has happened. Statistical associations underlying such theories need to be reasonably high. Correlations below 0.7 are, therefore, not very useful for predictive purposes in the social sciences. More will be said about this later in Chapter 6.

The reason theories need to be stronger for prediction purposes is this. If a theory fails to account satisfactorily for something which has

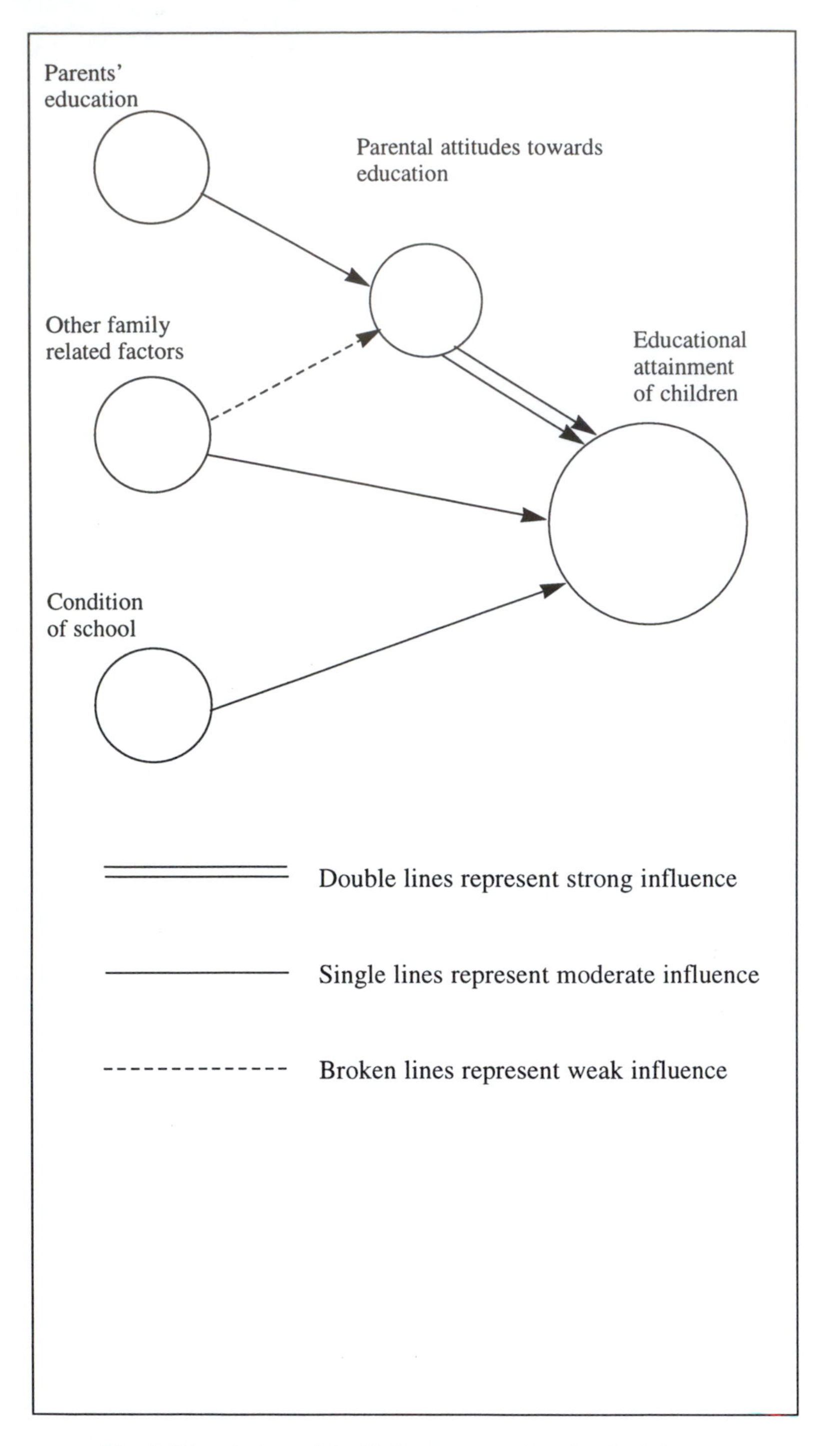

Fig. 3. Plowden's model of influences on educational attainment.

happened, investigations can be made to explain why the explanation did not fit the facts tidily, *ie* to supplement the explanation. Where prediction is concerned, however, it cannot be known in advance whether, or to what degree, the theory will fit the facts when the predicted event actually occurs.

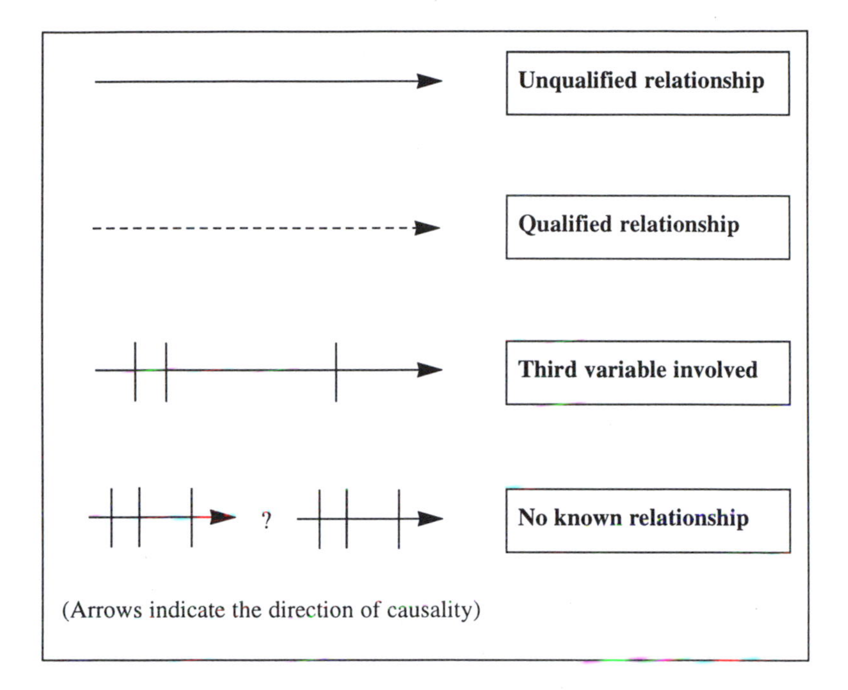

Fig. 4. Some examples of conventional ways of representing relationships in statements of theory.

SUMMARY

- Theory has a special meaning in science.
- A theory is different from a law.
- Theories are made of constructs.
- Strong theories can provide prediction; weak theories can only explain.

- Theories should be expressed in precise, preferably mathematical language.
- Physical scientists study things; social scientists study concepts.
- Concepts can be qualitative or quantitative.
- Models are possible ways things might relate to each other.
- Measures can differ in various ways (scales).
- Research can be inductive or deductive.
- Proceed in research by progressive focusing.
- The paradigms researchers work within shape the research they carry out.

QUESTIONS AND ANSWERS

1. *How can there be more than one theory about something? Surely they can't all be right.*

   Theories are different from laws. Laws explain things in *every* case, theories explain things in a *proportion* of cases.

   There are a number of reasons why different theories can co-exist. First, they may focus on different levels of analysis. For instance observational learning from exposure to television violence may explain aggression at a socio-psychological level, but it does not explain it at a psychobiological level. In the latter case we need to explain it in terms of physiological structures and neuro-chemicals.

   Secondly, the reason different theories may be required to explain different cases of the same thing may be that there is a missing link, or links, in the knowledge. Some day this may be discovered and the two or more theories reconciled as one.

   Thirdly, of course, some theories may simply be wrong; they may simply be erroneous explanations which, by chance, appear to fit the facts.

2. *Why is there so much jargon in scientific writing? Is it to baffle us with science?*

   Jargon should be kept to a minimum, but sometimes it is necessary in scientific writing because precise definition is important. The trouble is that many specialised terms are used in different ways. Readers should always ask themselves what this particular writer means by this particular term on this particular occasion.

3. *You say a concept is an idea existing only in the mind. 'House' is a concept and a house does not exist only in the mind, it exists in fact. You can see it, you can buy it, you can live in it.*

   Actual examples of the concept exist in the real world, but the actual essence of 'houseness', does not. That which causes us to categorise structures of widely different proportions and shapes – from the thatched cottage to the suburban mansion, from the igloo to the log cabin – all as houses is the concept itself. No house in the world contains all of these features.

4. *How can it ever be justifiable to base a research design on a theory of what you will find? Surely this is making a self-fulfilling prophecy.*

   Theory is always present; you can't get away from it. Better, perhaps, that it's scientific theory than unscientific theory.

CASE STUDIES

George seeks to develop a strong theory

A prominent model guiding George's thinking is Plowden's model of major influences in children's educational attainment. He considers that, since a child's attitude to education is a factor in its attainment level, then it may be significantly related to his family background. On the other hand, it could be mainly attributed to the unexplained influences in the model, but he feels the latter is unlikely. He seeks to test his hypothesis.

We can see, therefore, that his basic approach is deductive. George seeks to develop a strong theory, since his purpose is to provide data useful for spotting children at risk of underachievement. To achieve this his concepts need to be quantitative.

Graham uses established models

Being a cognitive psychologist restricts Graham's focus of interest to some degree. He excludes, for example, the physiological aspects of memory from his frame of reference, as indeed he does any psychoanalytical considerations of forgetting.

His research is deductive, by contrast with Sylvia's inductive research. Deductive research necessarily implies the existence of established theory.

There are a number of established models to guide his development of theory. Graham's research allows him to use ratio scales in his analyses. Ideally, he seeks to develop ever stronger theories.

Sylvia wants to generate theory

Sylvia works within a qualitative research paradigm. She tries, as much as possible, to prevent models guiding her research. Her aim is, instead, to generate theory, by induction, from the data she collects. She accepts, however, that complete avoidance of *a priori* use of models is impossible.

Sylvia's theories will be less precise than those of researchers working within empiricist paradigms. Many of her concepts will be qualitative in nature and the scales that she will use will often be of a nominal kind. Her theories are not designed to predict, but to describe. Consequently they are not necessarily strong theories.

DISCUSSION POINTS

1. How can there be several established theories about the same thing?

2. Take any area of knowledge and consider ways researchers from different paradigms would research the subject. Consider, also, the different kinds of conclusions which could be expected.

3. Consider some areas of knowledge where inductive research may be appropriate and others where deductive research might be more appropriate at present.

4. Should things that can't be measured ever be studied in the name of science?

3
Formulating Hypotheses

WHAT IS A HYPOTHESIS?

A hypothesis is a postulated connection between two or more variables. Hypotheses can be descriptive or causal.

Descriptive hypotheses postulate only an association, whereas causal hypotheses postulate a causal relationship.

SOURCES OF HYPOTHESES

There are a number of starting points from which to develop hypotheses; the more usual sources are as follows:

- expressing textual statement in terms of qualitative hypotheses
- looking for evidence to support, or challenge, a proposition/rival hypothesis
- chance occurrences
- cross classification data
- constant comparison of data, as new common factors are discovered.

The importance of testing other research

As will be explained in Chapter 8, it is important that a significant amount of research effort is devoted to testing the work of others, or testing your own previous findings. If you choose to use your research efforts in this way, you can simply take a hypothesis which was tested in another study and test it again using a different sample, perhaps from a different working universe (see page 56). Alternatively, you could use a different method.

Thirdly, you could consider whether there are other ways of interpreting the findings which the previous study had made, *ie* whether there are what we call 'rival hypotheses' which it had not adequately evaluated. You could, in fact, simply replicate, in every way, the work of that previous study; sometimes a change of researcher is enough to make the findings different. This is especially the case where relatively naturalistic methodology is concerned, for example in anthropological studies, where a researcher spends time with a particular community to try to make sense of their way of life. Different researchers will bring with them different preconceptions, attitudes and orientations and will, thus, focus on, respond to and interpret things in different ways.

Moving from qualitative to quantitative findings

Early research findings in any area of enquiry are likely to be qualitative in form. That is, they are less likely to be expressed in figures or any quantifiable form, which permits relatively precise comparisons and from which predictions can be made. The natural progression of science is towards ever increasing quantification of findings. It is useful, therefore, to take statements and findings expressed in qualitative form in studies to date and attempt to express them in quantitative form, so that they can be tested more precisely. The knowledge will, as a result, become more useful for explaining and predicting.

Stages of progressive quantification

There are various stages of progressive quantification:

- nominal scales
- ordinal scales
- interval scales
- ratio scales.

Nominal scales

Purely qualitative data is data presented according to a nominal scale, for example Catholic, Protestant, Jew, Muslim *etc*.

Ordinal scales

Ordinal scaling is organising concepts in terms of ranking. Child, adolescent, adult, for example, is data organised like this on the basis of age. The intervals between the categories are not equal.

Interval scales
Interval scaling amounts to ranking data in such a way that the intervals between each category are equal. IQ scores are an example of this. A weakness of this type of scaling is that it has no zero point.

Ratio scales
Ratio scales are the most advanced of all, for these are rankings with precise intervals and an exact zero point.

If findings to date are expressed only in qualitative terms, that is according to a nominal scale, it is worth trying to re-formulate them into a hypothesis which will give them ordinal scale properties. If they are presently expressed in ordinal scale terms then it will be useful to try to re-formulate them into a statement that has interval scale properties. If this is already the case then try to form a hypothesis which has ratio scale quality.

Studying exceptions to the rule
Studying exceptions to the rule can enhance understanding of the way something works. Now and again such exceptions come conspicuously to our attention. For example, a newspaper report of a person who performs amazing memory feats, recalling thousands of telephone numbers, is too good an opportunity to miss for a researcher working in an appropriate branch of memory research.

Cross-tabulating

Another means of formulating hypotheses is **cross-tabulation**. Supposing an educational researcher is studying underachievement and its causes, he or she may collect a variety of data by means of questionnaires. It may include achievement levels in various subjects and a variety of personal, home background, school and peer group factors. It might include whether the respondents were male or female, their parents' occupation, their social class, their area of residence, type of school, number of changes of school, amount of time spent on homework, attitudes to education held by friends, and so on.

This data may then be cross-tabulated, levels of achievement in each subject being plotted on the x axis and the other factors on the y axis. If a relatively large quantity stands out in any cell of the matrix this can provide the basis of a hypothesis to be tested. For example, if the amount of help and encouragement with homework was found to noticeably coincide with high levels of achievement in all areas, this would be grounds for formulating a hypothesis. As it happens this is one which had already been well tested.

SUMMARY

- Scientists formulate two hypotheses – a target and a null one. Then they test the null one.
- Science can never prove anything; it can only disprove things.
- Hypotheses can be descriptive or causal.
- There are various sources of hypotheses.

QUESTIONS AND ANSWERS

1. *Is hypothesising always appropriate?*

   No. In qualitative research it would defeat the object.

CASE STUDIES

George formulates a target and a null hypothesis

George has formulated a target hypothesis (H_1) that children's home background is associated with their attitude to education. His null hypothesis (H_0) is that there is no evidence that children's home background is associated with their attitude to education.

As we know, science can never prove anything; it can only disprove things. The best he can do, then, is to try to disprove that his hunch is incorrect and, thus, give reason to believe it *is* correct. Confusing as it at first seems, you'll get used to this way of thinking.

Graham formulates three hypotheses

Graham is pursuing a number of lines of enquiry on the subject of memory. For one of them he has formulated three hypotheses:

- H_1 that there is evidence of a single root factor of general memory.
- H_2 that there is evidence of two root factors of general memory.
- H_0 that there is no evidence of a single root factor or of two root factors of general memory.

Sylvia does not need a hypothesis

Sylvia's kind of research does not involve hypothesis testing, even of the descriptive kind. She seeks to keep as open a mind as possible as she records what she sees and hears. To formulate a hypothesis in advance would undermine this aim. She is not out to prove anything.

DISCUSSION POINTS

1. Suppose we are investigating the effect of classroom noise on achievement levels. We have set up a target hypothesis (H_1) that a relationship exists and a null hypothesis (H_0) that the target hypothesis is rejected. Suppose we decide that if a statistically significant correlation, above 0.7, is not found then the target hypothesis will be rejected. Is it justifiable to leave it there? Suppose a low correlation were found, say 0.2. Could this have an important meaning? Ought this to be explained?

2. If there is no scientific evidence that something exists, or that something happens, is it justifiable to say it does not exist or does not happen?

3. The stage in a project at which a hypothesis is formulated will influence the outcomes. Consider how this might be the case. Consider how the methods and the data might differ if:

   (a) a hypothesis was formulated *prior to* data collection
   (b) a hypothesis was formulated *during* data collection
   (c) a hypothesis was formulated *after* data collection.

4
Choosing a Method

USING EXPERIMENTS

An **experiment** is a means of testing the effect of one thing on another, or others.

Dependent and independent variables

The variable we are testing for its influence on the other one we call the **independent variable**. We call the other the **dependent variable**, because we want to see if its value is dependent upon the one being tested.

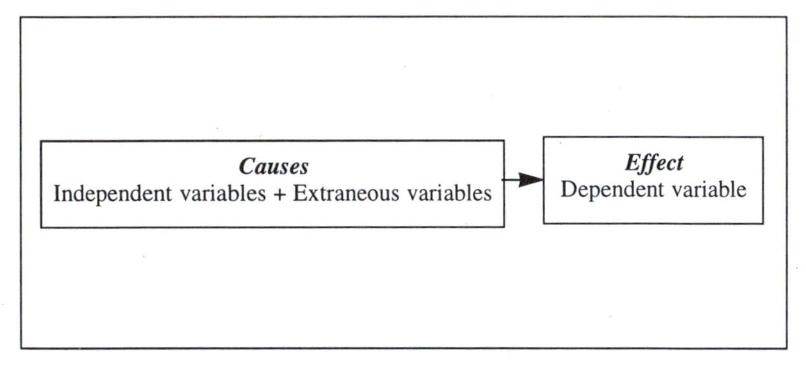

Fig. 5. The basic experimental formula.

Using a control group

In an experiment all known influences on the dependent variable are eliminated or held constant.

In the social sciences we cannot be sure we have not missed some of the influences. To allow for this we select a **control group** who will be tested for the same effect as the target group though the causal factor we are testing will be withheld. Since both groups will have been exposed to any influences we have missed, any difference in effect between the groups can be put down to the factor we are testing.

Random selection

It is important to randomly select which participants will be included in each group, *ie* the target group and the control group. This ensures that any difference in the outcomes will not be due to selection effects, *ie* differences of characteristics between the two groups. In Chapter 6 you will be shown how to randomly select a sample using random numbers generated by computer. An adequate way of randomly assigning half the sample to the target group and half to the control group, is to simply use odd numbers for one group and even numbers for the other.

ADVANTAGES AND DISADVANTAGES OF THE EXPERIMENTAL METHOD

Advantages

The main advantage of the experimental method is its suitability for testing causality. This is its essential function.

A second advantage is the degree of confidence we can have that the effect observed was caused by the thing tested. For this reason we say the experiment has high **internal validity**.

Disadvantages

The main disadvantage of the experimental method is that the behaviour of the phenomena observed takes places in very false circumstances. The laboratory is not like the real world. It is difficult to know how much the test can tell us about what would happen in the real world. Here other factors will influence the dependent variable in a whole host of ways. We therefore say the experimental method has low **external validity**, which means it is not very generalisable to situations in the real world.

TYPES OF EXPERIMENT

Classical design

In the classical design a randomly selected target group and control group are tested in respect of the value of the dependent variable present. This process is known as **pre-test**. The target group is then exposed to the independent variable. The value of the dependent variable is then measured again for the two groups and any change is attributed to the effect of the independent variable.

Control group design without pre-testing

This is the classical design except that pre-testing is omitted. Pre-testing can introduce bias since the effect of being studied or having been studied can change people's behaviour.

The Hawthorne effect
Students of business studies may already be aware of the effects Elton Mayo found in his work at the Hawthorne Works. When researchers become interested in people they begin acting differently and the changes can continue even after the researchers have gone. This has come to be known as the **Hawthorne effect**. In the wider research context the effects of being tested are referred to as **reactive effects of measures** and will be dealt with more fully in Chapter 7.

The practice effect
Furthermore, being tested makes a participant a more skilled testee. A person whose IQ has already been tested a number of times could be expected to score slightly higher than another whose IQ has not. This is often known as the **practice effect** and this can apply to the experimental situation, too.

Disadvantage of not pre-testing
A disadvantage of this method is that the two groups are not pre-tested prior to the experiment. We cannot, therefore, be sure they were equivalent when the experiment started. The next design to be dealt with allows for this.

Solomon four-group experimental design

This is a combination of the classical design and the control group design without pre-test. Two target groups and two control groups are selected and one of each is tested by each method. This way we can be sure of the initial equivalence of the target and control group and the effects of pre-testing can be ruled out.

Factorial designs

Sometimes we may suspect more than one independent variable to be responsible for changes in a dependent variable. Furthermore, such influences may work together in some way so that their combined effect is greater or lesser, or simply different, to the effect of either on their own.

An experiment which seeks to test a number of causal factors, singly and in combination, is known as a **factorial design**. These can follow the lines of the classical, the control group without pre-test, or the Solomon four design. They are different only in so far as more independent variables are involved.

Matching control groups

The purpose of randomising the selection of target and control groups is to make each as equivalent as possible. There are sometimes ways of improving randomisation in this respect.

Supposing 60 per cent of the sample are female, randomisation will not ensure equivalence between the groups in terms of sex. If this is highly relevant to the test then two groups can be selected initially in a non-random way to reflect the equivalence in this quality. Each member of each group could then be assigned to either the target group or the control group by means of the toss of a coin.

Allowing for biases

Bias in experiments can never be completely ruled out. The nature of experimenters, themselves, may, for example, influence the way participants apply themselves to the tasks required. They may act differently, for example, if the experimenter is young and of the opposite sex to themselves than they would otherwise. A casually dressed experimenter with an easygoing personality may make participants more relaxed than a stern-looking experimenter in a pin-stripe suit. Participants may infer, from the appearance and manner of experimenters, the kinds of outcomes they are expecting. As will be explained in Chapter 7, participants often have a tendency to give researchers what they think they want. This is known as **experimenter modelling effect**.

Minimising experimenter effects

Experimenter effects can never be completely removed but steps can be taken to minimise them.

- Different experimenters may be used for different stages of an experiment, or for different sub-groups. In the latter case their allocation may be randomly selected.

- The researcher may employ an uninformed colleague to carry out the experiments without really understanding what the researcher expects to find.

- Knowledge of whether a group is a target group or a control group can be withheld from those carrying out the experiments. As a result, they will not know what to expect and will not be able to unwittingly communicate it in any way to the participants.

- Participants can simply be urged to behave as normally as possible, as if they were not taking part in an experiment.

- The experiment can be designed so that participants are not aware that it is an experiment, or it can be designed so that they are unaware the experiment has started yet.

QUASI EXPERIMENTS

Multiple time series

Some of the effects observed may not be due to the independent variable focused upon.

Example

Suppose a researcher wished to study the way international conflict affects patriotism. He may notice that an independent variable indicator has been thrown up by chance when one country declared war on another. An increase in the popularity of the country's nationalist political parties recorded immediately after a declaration of war (consider, for example, the Falklands crisis) may have something to do with that event. However, some of the increase in patriotism may be due to other causes, such as a growing level of affluence in the country and falling unemployment.

The degree to which the observed effect is due to these could, perhaps, be measured in another way. We could do this by taking soundings of patriotism levels in two countries whose recent pattern of economic development is similar, but one of which is not involved in an international conflict. The degree of increase in patriotism in the latter country may then be assumed to be that degree of change which would have occurred in the target country had the international conflict not arisen.

Using a non-equivalent control group

Sometimes it is possible to approximate quite closely to experimental conditions.

Example

Suppose we wanted to assess the influence of short-sightedness on educational achievement. We could compare the educational progress between two points in time for a random sample of normal-sighted and visually handicapped children. Though each would be randomly selected, there would not be random assignment to target and control groups as there would be in a true experiment. We cannot, after all, randomly select who is visually handicapped and who is not. The other major weakness of this, by comparison with a true experiment, is that it is difficult to know and assess all the possible influences on those children's educational progress.

Control group pre-test, target group post-test design

Sometimes it is useful to compare a population which has been exposed to something with another which has not. Anti-nuclear campaigners cite comparisons between levels of childhood leukaemia found in the general population and those found in the vicinity of a nuclear power station. The control group has been pre-tested, for it has been tested before exposure to the close proximity of a nuclear power station. Indeed, such exposure might never affect it. The target group, however, has already been exposed to this effect and so the measurements taken there must be regarded as post-testing, *ie* testing after exposure.

This kind of design lends itself to other studies of environmental effects on health, for example the effects of an aluminium source in an area. Similarly, the effects of lead in the atmosphere might be studied using a target group of people living near Birmingham's Spaghetti Junction. A control group might be selected from people living on the island of Sark, where there are no roads to speak of.

Advantage and disadvantages

One of the main advantages of this method is that it avoids testing effects. The main disadvantage is that it is difficult to be sure that none of the control group have at any time been part of the target group and exposed to the stimuli under focus. A Sark islander, for example, may have travelled in a traffic congested country and may, indeed, have visited Spaghetti Junction.

Randomising allocation

Sometimes it may be possible to randomise the allocation of participants into the target and control groups. Suppose, for example, policy makers wanted to study the effect on health of fluoridation of water supplies. Communities could be picked at random to have their water supplies fluoridated. Their health could then be measured after fluoridation and compared with the health of those who live in communities where fluoridation has not taken place.

Interrupted time series

Quasi-experiments are methods which approximate to experimentation but do not fit all the requirements of that definition. Usually the experimenter has no control in respect of exposing the target group to the independent variable. Invariably this occurs as a chance of fate. Unusually hot summers or unusually cold winters could be treated as the independent variable to measure the effect of temperature on certain dependent variables, conflict behaviour among people for example. Civil war can be used as an independent variable to measure the effect of stress on the health or behaviour of populations.

This design is called the **interrupted time series design**, because behaviour before the circumstances focused upon interrupted the pattern is compared with behaviour afterwards.

USING THE SURVEY METHOD

In the social sciences a survey involves collecting information from a large number of people. The data may be elicited face to face (interviewing) or at a distance (by postal questionnaires).

There are various types of interview. Each has its strengths and weaknesses.

Structured interviews

Interviews may be structured to varying degrees. At one end of the spectrum an interview may differ from a questionnaire survey only in so far as the researcher, rather than the participant, completes the form. At the other end of the spectrum the interviewer uses an **interview schedule**. This is merely a list of themes to be dealt with.

Ethnographic style interviewing

Ethnographic style interviews are highly unstructured. The rationale is that structuring the interview imposes the researcher's frame of reference on the data to be generated. A participant's world view, as seen through their own frame of reference, will not be recorded by the interviewer. Life treats people in different ways and life determines the way people structure and interpret their experiences.

Consider a researcher from a middle class background seeking to understand what it is like to be homeless by interviewing people who sleep on the streets. He will fail to do so if he sets his questions in advance and lacks awareness of the way his background will distort what he is seeing and hearing. The latter is known as **phenomenological bias** and will be dealt with in Chapter 7.

Tapping the interviewee's world view
Rather than having a prepared list of questions it would be preferable to begin by saying to the participant:

> 'If I want to understand your day-to-day life what questions ought I ask you?'

It will be the interviewee, then, who will say which themes in his experience are most prominent and relevant; it will be the interviewee who provides the list of questions. Priorities are very different for the two – the financially comfortable, well-housed interviewer and the penniless, and perhaps hungry and cold inhabitant of cardboard city.

Using a questionnaire

Questionnaires may be made up of **open-ended questions, closed-ended.questions**, or a mixture of both.

The open-ended question
An open-ended question is one which does not limit the answer to a 'yes', a 'no' or a range of set alternatives, *eg* red, green or yellow. Participants can answer the question any way they like. An advantage of this kind of question is that it does not threaten to bias the findings by imposing a frame of reference, effectively limiting the way the participant may answer. The main disadvantage is that the completed forms will be difficult to analyse and the researcher will, in the end, impose such a frame of reference on the answers in order to classify them.

The closed-ended question
Closed-ended questions have the opposite advantages and disadvantages. They impose a direct threat to the validity of the findings. They represent not so much what the participant wanted to say as what the participant was forced to choose from out of the alternatives given. Closed-ended questions may be of **binary choice** or **multiple choice** type. An example of multiple choice questions commonly found is those which conform to the Likert method of scaling, for example:

Strongly approve/Approve/Neutral/Disapprove/Strongly disapprove

or

Strongly like/Like/Indifferent/Dislike/Strongly dislike

Yet another kind of multiple choice question asks participants to rank-order a number of items. An example might be: Evaluate the order of importance to you of the following items:

- income
- friends
- family
- peace of mind
- the respect of others.

Quintamensional questionnaire design

This kind of question structuring was first introduced by Gallow in 1947. It is useful in studying attitudes and opinions. Open-ended questions are formulated to elicit awareness of the issue in question and general attitudes towards it. A closed-ended question follows to capture information on specific attitudes to the subject. An open-ended question is placed next to explore the participants' justifications for their attitudes. This is followed by a closed-ended question to tap the intensity with which they hold such attitudes. The closed-ended questions are typically of the multiple choice type described earlier:

Strongly approve/Approve/Indifferent/Disapprove/Strongly disapprove

Dos and don'ts of questionnaire design

Do

- Use plain English.
- Estimate the lowest educational standard likely to feature in your sample and pitch your language at that level.
- Begin with some easy questions.
- Move through the topic logically and consistently.

- Make the questionnaire look professional and attractive. Research shows appearance is related to response rate.

Do not

- Use ambiguous terms.
- Jump from topic to topic.
- Use leading questions, *eg* 'Do you think your teachers misunderstood you?'
- Use stereotypes.
- Cite a popular view on an issue as a preamble to the question, *eg* 'Press reports are claiming that the *feel good factor* is returning to the market place. Would you be more prepared to take on a mortgage today than you would have been a year ago?'
- Use abstract concepts such as a 'sense of community', 'power', 'alienation' *etc.*

Conducting interviews

Do

- Try to put the interviewee at ease.
- Be attentive.
- Show interest.
- Be sympathetic.
- Probe gently for more information when necessary.

Do not

- Use leading questions.
- Rush the interviewee.
- Finish the interviewee's sentences for him/her.

The information given here provides a general picture to enable readers to decide whether to use the survey methodology. If they decide to do so they may obtain more detailed information in some of the specialist works listed at the end of this book.

USING OBSERVATION METHODS

Observation methods can be passive or involve participation.

- In passive observation researchers just watch and record.
- In active observation researchers get involved in the group behaviour. We call this **participant observation**. This may be overt or covert, depending on whether researchers disclose why they have joined the group.

Participant observation

An advantage of participant observation is that researchers can 'get behind the veil'. They can become accepted as members of the group being studied, so the members cease to show them only the behaviour they wish them to see as researchers. In other words, a participant observer is more likely to see people behaving naturally.

This is especially so if their true purpose for joining the group is not disclosed. This is known as **covert research**. This type of method poses an obvious ethical dilemma. Nevertheless, many covert research projects are carried out and researchers considering this method will have to handle the ethical question themselves. One way of handling it is by asking themselves whether the behaviour they intend to study is normally displayed publically, without reservation, so that anyone who may read the report could have actually seen for themselves the behaviour on which it is based.

Advantages of observation

Observational techniques have their advantages. They are useful for a wide range of research problems and the data quality benefits because of the absence of **testing effects** (see Chapter 7). If people know they are being observed you can expect them to behave differently from the way they would otherwise.

Disadvantages of observation

There are disadvantages to observational methodology too. First, **reliability** tends to be lower.

- Reliability of findings is the degree to which we can expect other research projects using the same methodology to arrive at the same findings.

No two people see the world in exactly the same ways; each brings to the scene different preconceptions, prejudices and preferences. Each will be looking through different lenses, so to speak. Each will interpret what they see differently.

These effects can, to some degree, be offset by providing a common structure for researchers to use and a set of interpretation criteria on what to look for and how to make judgements.

Validity of findings

The findings from observational methodology tend to have relatively low **validity**.

- Validity is the degree to which what we are recording or measuring is what we set out to record or measure.

Example

Researchers observing classroom interaction will be recording their view and interpretation of what is taking place, as filtered and modified by the knowledge, understanding, preconceptions, prejudices and evaluations they brought with them to the scene of observation. There could be any degree of divergence between what was actually taking place, and what the observers thought they saw and wrote down.

Using several observers

Sometimes more than one observer will be used to watch the same set of behaviour. Their measurements and recordings will then be compared and an **interscorer reliability coefficient** computed. If fewer than half the measurements are comparable then interscorer reliability is certainly very low and findings highly suspect.

Going native

Another important disadvantage of observational methods applies where participant observation methodology is used. This is where a researcher actually joins a community, perhaps without disclosing that he has joined to study it. The problem is that of 'going native', a term traditionally used by the Foreign Office for when a British consul starts to see things through the eyes of the people of the host country. It becomes difficult for that person to remain objective and see things in terms of the way they affect his own country.

The same applies to community researchers and anthropologists. The frequently quoted statement of Whyte, in his paper *Street Corner Society*, sums it all up. The participant observer, he points out:' . . . starts out as a non-participating observer and ends as a non-observing participant.'

Coaction

Another disadvantage of observational methods is that they do not enable researchers to easily distinguish interaction from **coaction**. Coaction simply refers to the fact that two people are acting in response to, or directing a communication towards, each other. It is only interaction when the action of one influences the action of the other. In addition, the interaction between two parties may be influenced by the fact that others are present. Observational methods may miss this detail, while retrospective interviewing may be able to tap it.

Conversely, it may appear that one person is communicating with another, but that person may intend their words and behaviour to be seen and heard by others in the group. This methodology may fail to pick this up, while methods like retrospective interviewing or questionnaires would.

Instruments for structured observation

To make their studies replicable observers have to use standard criteria on what to attend to and how to code it. Quite a number of systems have been developed. Readers intending to use this methodology will find Simon and Boyer's (1974) *Anthology of Instruments for Observational Research* a useful source of reference.

Researchers using structured observation techniques tend to be interested in the following things:

- measure
- form
- duration
- frequency
- antecedent conditions
- consequences.

Form is the type of interaction taking place, or the target phenomena. Researchers may, for example, be interested in instances of agreement behaviour, or rapid blinking, as an indication of anxiety. Researchers are interested in the duration of each type of phenomena focused upon and the frequency with which it occurs. They are also interested in what precedes and follows it, because these facts may enable them to explain the phenomena in question and predict its consequences.

Behaviourial categories in observation

The things which researchers working in observational paradigms tend to be interested in can be categorised into:

- linguistic behaviour
- extra-linguistic behaviour
- non-verbal behaviour
- spatial behaviour.

Extra-linguistic behaviour

Amplitude and pitch of speech can provide useful information about what is actually going on in a group situation. There are instruments which can be used to record this, such as speech spectrometers.

Researchers find it useful to calculate a **speech disturbance ratio** (Mahl 1959). Examples of disturbances in speech include:

- repetitions
- incomplete sentences
- slips of the tongue.

These are added together and divided by the total words spoken and this figure gives a measure of the level of anxiety present.

The level of continuity of speech, *ie* continuity without interruptions or hesitations, is another thing which researchers find of interest.

Verbal style and language quality can also provide useful information. Examples of what researchers may focus on include:

- dialect
- redundant words
- typical expression used.

Such things can give indications of social class, level of education and state of mind.

Focusing on body language

Different kinds of **body language** can be of interest to researchers. The face provides information on emotional states while the body position can provide information on the intensity of those states. If a situation is video recorded and the videotape slowed down, information otherwise unavailable will be revealed. Minute eye movements may be detected, for example, when something untrue is said.

Leventhal and Sharp (1965) devised a system of symbols for rapidly noting different kinds of observed effect. Movements and their interpretation, for example, are coded as follows.

- -	=	comfort
◡̲◡̲	=	minor discomfort
\ /	=	major discomfort

There are many more symbols in their scheme, the full bibliographical reference of which is given at the end of this book.

Body language like asymmetry of limbs indicates relaxation. Rapid movement of feet, hands or head can indicate stress and self-caressing behaviour, such as leg hugging, can indicate insecurity.

Equipment for recording behaviour

There is a wide variety of equipment now available for recording behaviour for observation; the most common examples are tape recorders, still cameras and video cameras.

CONSIDERING QUALITATIVE RESEARCH

Sometimes researchers seek to understand, rather than to explain or predict behaviour. This is the case particularly when an area of enquiry is in its infancy.

In this kind of research it is important for researchers to try, as much as possible, to see things through the eyes of the people they are studying. They have to try to put aside their own values, prejudices and preferences. If they don't they will distort what they see by forcing it to fit to their own frame of reference. The people they are studying may not have the same focus, may not see the same things as important, or evaluate things in the same way.

Generating grounded theory

It is difficult to analyse and interpret qualitative data, but a common method is one called **grounded theory generation**. This involves letting the data itself suggest a theory, rather than beginning with theory and looking to see if the data fits it.

There are obvious validity problems associated with this type of research. It often aims to understand the world view of members of a culture, or sub-culture, to which the researcher does not belong. It will be difficult for researchers not to interpret the data in terms of their own way of looking at the world, that is, their own **phenomenology**.

Improving the validity of qualitative research

There are ways of improving validity for this kind of data, however. One of the ways is **phenomenological validation**. The researcher declares all of the influences in their biography which may have affected their interpretation of the data. The researcher's social class background and their political affiliations, will have affected the way they interpret the data. Males will tend to see things differently to females, so the sex and gender of the individual will affect the interpretation too. The scientific paradigm within which the researcher was trained must also be declared. This, too, will have coloured the way the observations were understood. The personal experiences of the researcher will have had their effect too. A person who has, in the past, been mugged by juvenile delinquents may be expected to interpret juvenile delinquent behaviour differently from someone who has never had such an experience.

Another way of validating qualitative findings is presenting the report to the people studied and asking them if the researcher has got it right.

STRENGTHS AND WEAKNESSES OF DIFFERENT METHODS

Experimentation

Strengths

- Can test for cause and effect.
- High objectivity.

Weaknesses

- Often difficult to design for social phenomena.
- Difficulty in isolating independent variables.

- Independent variables cannot always be randomly assigned
- Ethical problems
- Range of subject matter amenable to this method is sometimes argued to be trivial, or of doubtful relevance.

Quasi-experiments

Strengths

- Not as artificial as experimentation and, therefore, offers higher external validity.
- Absence of testing effects.
- Ethical advantages – no need to deceive the participants.

Weaknesses

- Lack of control over independent variables. Significant control can only be achieved by means of expensive design.
- Low internal validity.
- Even where a control group is used there is no certainty that it may not have become polluted with target group members.
- Many alternative hypotheses, which all have to be examined.
- History effects (interrupted time series design).

Surveys

Strengths

- Can collect lots of data.
- Can tap attitudes and beliefs.
- Data comes ready structured and, therefore, needs less analysis.

Weaknesses

- Truth of answers may be suspect
- Memory decay
- Insensitive
- Interviewer and questionnaire bias
- Depends heavily on participant motivation.

Observation methods

Strengths

- Better quality data than retrospective interview accounts.
- Adaptable to many research problems.
- Can be used in combination with experimentation.
- Can tap data which may not be available by survey methods, *eg* where the participants are relatively inarticulate and not very introspective (*eg* children).
- Can reveal unexpected variable relationships.

Weaknesses

- Low reliability.
- Low validity.
- Presence of observer changes people's behaviour.

Qualitative methods

Strengths

- Relevance of findings.

- Useful if seeking to understand rather than explain or predict.
- Sensitive.

Weaknesses

- Low reliability.
- Low validity.
- Time-consuming.
- Expensive.
- Low objectivity.

SUMMARY

- Research can be quantitative or qualitative.
- Methods used can be categorised in terms of: experimentation, quasi-experimentation, surveys and observation.
- There are various designs within each of these categories.
- Two main advantages of experimentation are that it is useful for investigating causality and that the findings have high internal validity.
- A major disadvantage of experimentation is that findings have low external validity.
- The main advantage of surveys is that the findings have high external validity.
- The main disadvantages of surveys is that the findings have low internal validity.
- Observational methodology is useful for many types of study and it has the advantage of reduced testing effects.
- Major disadvantages of observational methodology are that

findings have low reliability and validity, and observers may miss subjective meanings of behaviour.

QUESTIONS AND ANSWERS

1. *It seems the kinds of things that can be made amenable to experimentation are rather trivial. The really useful kinds of social knowledge could not be reduced to a laboratory situation. Is this correct?*

   This is often argued. It is known as the rigour versus relevance debate.

2. *What is a 'natural experiment'?*

   Another name for a quasi-experiment.

3. *The really important questions concern human welfare – the effects of pollution and work practices, etc – but how can you study these, for you would have to permit people to suffer?*

   That is the purpose of the quasi-experiment. Another way is to use an **ex-post facto research** design. This means 'after the fact'. In this kind of research you are studying the evidence of what has already happened.

4. *How do you know people will tell the truth in questionnaires? They might seek to mischievously mislead.*

   All methods are based on assumptions. The questionnaire is based on the assumption that people tend to tell the truth. Yes, there may be some who will seek to undermine the research, but if this assumption was not reasonable then questionnaire research would yield widely different findings to other kinds of research in the same area. This is not shown to be the case.

5. *If an observer comes into a class all the children will be on their best behaviour, so the researcher won't see the normal situation.*

   Yes, but as will be explained in Chapter 8, it is important to study things from a variety of standpoints. This includes using a variety of methods. The difference between the combined findings of other methods and those of the observational method can reasonably be attributed to this problem and to other specific biases of the observation method, *eg* observers' subjectivity. Allowances can, therefore, be made for the distortion.

6. *Researchers seeking to study people's experiences acknowledge that those experiences will always be unique to the people they are studying. How, then, can this be building useful scientific knowledge?*

   This is a reasonable observation. It is arguable that this kind of research is more an art than a science, if art is defined as the presentation of new ideas, or old ideas in new ways. Such a presentation of unique, personal experience in the form of a document, carefully produced to represent the true experience as closely as possible, relatively free of the compiler's own interpretation, is, perhaps, as much a representation of an original idea in a new way as is a picture which seeks to represent a physical landscape in the form of a decorated, flat canvas.

   What do practitioners themselves say about this?

   With regard to the doubt that his kind of research can ever produce useful knowledge, some practitioners of this methodology themselves share this doubt. Indeed, some authoritative users of such methodology now doubt the possibility of discovering valid social knowledge at all, since it is not objective in its nature. It is constructed by those who hold it from an interaction of what they experience with their own personal biographical situation and psychological make-up.

   Worse still, when it is communicated to, or observed by, a researcher this whole reconstruction process is compounded, because the researcher's personal standpoint creeps into the interaction between the research subject and the researcher.

   It is reasonable to assume, therefore, that what comes out of such a study is not even a representation of an idea in a new form, but an original product of the whole process of the research. If so, this fits the other definition of art – the representation of new ideas.

   So is art useful? The artists would argue that the value of art lies in making us think in new ways. They don't have to be useful ways, they just have to expand our consciousness.

   Researchers in this area often admit they may not be able to produce true representations. However, they tend to evaluate their work on the basis of whether it generates new questions and whether it will persuade anyone to change their beliefs. Again, this would, arguably, qualify it as an art, rather than a science, which one would tend to think of as something which seeks to *explain* and *predict* rather than to describe. Then again, some speak of **descriptive sciences**.

Qualitative researchers might argue that their methodology is scientific because it uses clearly defined methods to aid replication. Fine artists, however, do this too; they have their specific techniques, which they describe, publicise and which are taught in art schools. This does not make them scientists.

So why do qualitative researchers cling to the identity of scientists?

It could lie in the fact that science is seen as somehow more prestigious than art. I am not going to pronounce upon this debate. What I will say, though, is that, science or art, it can still be regarded as research and, as such, is a proper subject for this book to speak about.

CASE STUDIES

George uses survey methodology for high external validity

George's research is quantitative. He uses survey methodology, comprising attitude scales and a questionnaire. The questionnaire contains both open-ended and closed-ended questions and is completed by an interviewer in each case. He also uses an 'educationally relevant home background' index that he has devised.

George's purpose is to influence national educational policy. Consequently, he needs a method which offers high external validity – findings which are highly generalisable to the general population. Survey methodology fulfils this requirement.

The degree to which his data will have internal validity, though, depends on the care with which he has designed his questionnaire and his attitude scale. It also depends on the care with which he analyses his data to his home background index.

Graham uses experimentation and questionnaires

Graham's research is also quantitative. The main methodology used is experimentation, structured according to a factorial design, comparing target and control groups without pre-testing. A control group is employed, but because of the nature of one of the independent variables (99th percentile IQ level), random assignment to the control group is not possible. It is impossible to selectively apply this independent variable, being, as it is, a personal attribute of the participants themselves.

Questionnaires are also used in this study, containing a number of open- and closed-ended questions to provide supporting data.

Sylvia uses ethnographic-style interviewing

Sylvia's research is qualitative. She seeks to describe and understand. Her methodology tends to be less rigorous and more naturalistic than that of George or Graham. It is argued that rigorous methods would be too insensitive to obtain the kind of data she is seeking. Her aim is grounded theory generation. She collects data, tries to make some kind of sense out of it – some kind of naive theory – by induction. Then she collects more data to test and extend that theory, and so the process goes on.

Much of Sylvia's data is collected using ethnographic style interviewing. She tends to begin an interview, for example, by asking: 'If I want to understand how you see the world, what sort of questions should I be asking you?'

Consequently, she taps the frames of reference of her subjects, rather than seeking to understand their outlooks directly from her own frame of reference.

DISCUSSION POINTS

1. Some social scientists feel that only knowledge which can be pursued with scientifically rigorous methodology is worth pursuing. Others argue that the kinds of facts that are amenable to rigorous methodology are of little value when discovered. Although less reliable and less valid, the facts which can be pursued with less rigorous methodology are more useful. What is your view on this?

2. Can you think of examples of facts which fall into these two categories?

3. Try to think of some event, which you have read about in the papers, which could have provided valuable information not accessible in any other way.

4. Consider the kind of detail which a passive observer might miss.

5. In what areas of inquiry do you think observation methodology is useful?

6. Have you ever filled in a questionnaire? Did you find it difficult choosing between options?

7. Were you completely happy with the choices you made?

8. It is known that the appearance of a questionnaire affects the response rate. Try to remember the appearance of the questionnaire you filled in.

9. Do you normally respond to questionnaires when you receive them? If not, why not? Are there some you respond to and others to which you do not? Why is this?

5
Sampling

WHY SAMPLE?

One reason for sampling is that it's often unfeasible to study all the people or things which have the qualities we are interested in. The funding may not be available for such a large operation. Logistically, it might be difficult, too. It may be almost impossible to locate everyone concerned and a nightmare to coordinate such a big project even if we could.

A good example is shopping behaviour. It would be unthinkable to question everyone who goes shopping. Instead we take a sample, and if we do it right it will give us a good picture of the behaviour of the general population.

Another reason is that sampling is often more accurate than studying all the people, or things, in which we're interested. This may, at first, appear difficult to accept. However, the larger the project the more administration errors can occur in the coordinating and analysing of the data.

USING WORKING UNIVERSES

Often we do not know who all the people we are interested in *are*, or where we can find them. We may only have knowledge of small groups of them. These are known as **working universes** as opposed to the **general universe**. The latter refers to all the people, or things, with the quality we are interested in.

As an example, if we want to study superior memory ability we cannot know who all the people with outstanding memories are. However, we can locate those who take part, and do well, in memory challenges.

Another reason for using working universes is that our funds are likely to be limited. Data collection and analysis costs money and those who provide the funding do not have bottomless purses.

The danger of bias

The trouble is that working universes will not necessarily be representative of the whole population of people we are interested in, so our findings may be biased. We have to assess by whatever means are available how closely they do match.

Example
Consider, again, the example of a study of people with superior memory. It was suggested we could study people who had done well in memory challenges. It is unlikely that everyone with superior memory will take part in such events. There will be things about this group which will predispose them to do so. This will make them different from the rest. However, as we study more and more working universes we will build a picture which conforms more and more closely to the general universe.

RANDOM AND NON-RANDOM SAMPLING

A random sample is one where each person or thing in a population has a known chance of being chosen. An example is the selection of bingo balls at a bingo hall. The National Lottery numbers are selected in the same way. Screwing raffle tickets up and placing them in a hat for somebody to pick a winning number follows the same principle, though it's a very crude method, for some tickets will stick together. Scientists tend to use **random numbers lists**, or computer programs, for generating random numbers.

Purposive samples

If a sample is not randomly selected it is called a **purposive** sample. In a purposive sample the chances of any element being selected are either unknown or guaranteed to be 0 per cent or 100 per cent.

Advantages and disadvantages of sampling types

Each type of sampling strategy has its advantages and disadvantages. Purposive samples can provide better descriptive data, while random samples are better if you are seeking to explain or predict something rather than describe its nature. Purposive samples tend to be used in the early stages of any branch of knowledge, for here the focus is on describing what later researchers will seek to explain.

Random sampling

When we speak of random sampling we are including varying degrees of randomness. The distinction has already been made, for example, between the randomness of selecting bingo balls from a machine and picking tickets out of a hat. Here are some of the variations on random sampling:

Pure random sampling
Where every element has an equal chance of being chosen.

Systematic sampling
Where every nth number is selected, *eg* every 10th house. (See Fig. 6.)

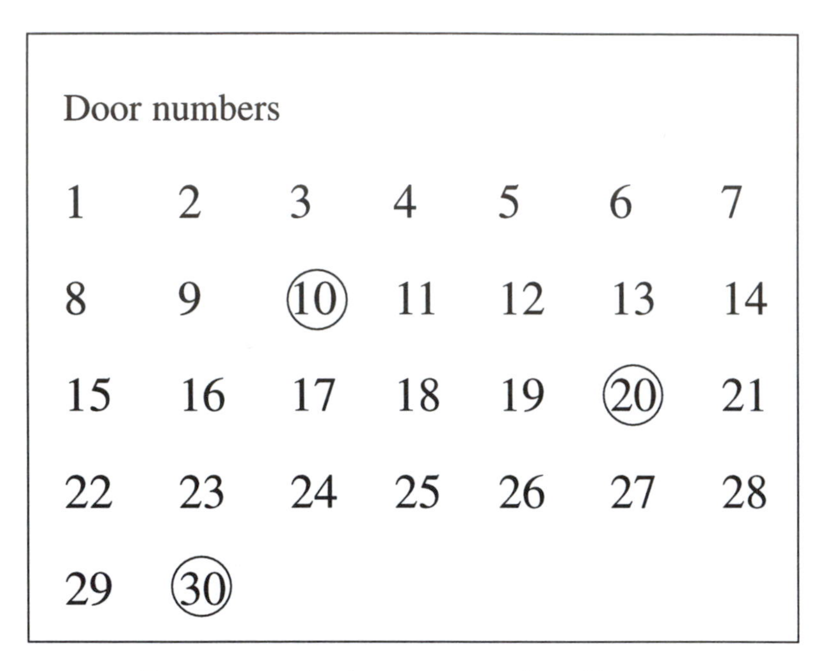

Fig. 6. An example of systematic sampling, taking every 10th door number of a street.

Cluster sampling
This is where samples are taken of clusters of the population. For example the health of workers on an industrial estate might be studied by taking a sample from each factory.

Stratified cluster sampling
This is cluster sampling, but allowing for varying sizes of the clusters. For example if one factory is twice as large as another the sample taken from it will also be twice as large.

Purposive sampling

There are four types of purposive sample:

- **heterogeneous**
- **homogeneous**
- **structural**
- **haphazard**.

.4703925	.7990661	.8832613	.4076671	.9583889	.7986162	.8270244	.3780452
.2556445	.9555662	.4457716	.7214551	.1818913	.7364126	.0515696	.4461969
.7746076	.8259458	.2432195	.4024332	.3041535	.0191907	.3988333	.8541683
.7710392	.3798944	.4868062	.8507769	.3471161	.3895089	.6886145	.0768156
.6019495	.2436876	.4609501	.6187602	.3450193	.1274124	.9265529	.8191126
.3890701	.6337634	.2204196	.5524524	.0565474	.0684246	.5530718	.1339738
.7467276	.3409520	.6189998	.3749706	.8713287	.9160909	.5113570	.9196260
.9532509	.1563613	.5451654	.1456693	.2086655	.0831832	.3978949	.7368664
.1082983	.5372861	.1607623	.0952864	.9107947	.8493432	.1678998	.9874784
.4347971	.3496395	.7049367	.1170823	.6352929	.4116164	.4520494	.5061800
.2724985	.0623070	.7883741	.5467614	.3451809	.1476184	.4522994	.5374277
.1784649	.3081085	.5135664	.1958041	.4755120	.4389964	.8745477	.3184669
.8083580	.0447471	.5933886	.1735757	.6969673	.1209100	.1137543	.2192824
.4102953	.2869148	.8643489	.0436131	.4516339	.4542345	.7793182	.4147800
.8474964	.9370511	.1313832	.4228956	.8619524	.7440551	.0068829	.8603631
.5453928	.1741007	.7625920	.3239983	.4997867	.4733344	.1667969	.8496128
.2016062	.2007812	.0976503	.2062847	.7855921	.1990131	.8766363	.5795352
.4418971	.2371376	.6422059	.2757346	.4668288	.3535959	.1994912	.9364048
.0506040	.3254975	.6871837	.8979570	.2446224	.5778050	.2256217	.2027092
.3386467	.3308411	.3551430	.3928785	.1098107	.7263371	.7921385	.0173103
.1637825	.4728072	.1009040	.6129970	.6246227	.0778434	.7304273	.3034122
.9265204	.8150445	.8805680	.0710052	.8756521	.4565112	.0639006	.9875728
.4465988	.8248543	.1067845	.3480563	.5070344	.3792951	.4118832	.4853982
.6747793	.3474168	.4271045	.3880677	.5084595	.5574384	.6798033	.9754113
.9264124	.8015441	.1930117	.1264672	.8084016	.0502009	.2751166	.2055784

If the number of people or things in a population runs into 3 digits then just read off consecutive 3-digit numbers, working row-wise or clock-wise, from any arbitrarily chosen starting point. For example, starting at row 2, column 3, there would be 445, 771, 672, 145 and so on.

Fig. 7. Example of a list of random numbers generated by computer.

Heterogeneous samples

These are selected from people or things which are in some way alike in a relevant detail. For example, if we were studying adaptability by means of heterogeneous samples, we might take a sample of people with proven, high perseverance quality, such as Duke of Edinburgh Gold Award holders, or a sample of people with known high IQ.

Another kind of heterogeneous sampling is **quota sampling**. This is an attempt to match the sample to the general population on a number of dimensions. For example, to study the attitudes to work of employees in a firm you might assess the proportions of males to females, ethnic groupings, or age groups and then select a sample which reflected these. If there were twice as many females as males in the firm then you would sample twice as many women as men, and so on.

Homogeneous samples

There are two types of homogeneous sample: those containing **extreme cases** and those made up of **rare cases**.

- In extreme case sampling we are selecting people with a quality which lies at the top or bottom of the range of such qualities found in the general population. For instance, in studying human fitness we may select only Olympic medallists.

- Rare case samples are those which contain a quality, or qualities, found only rarely. An example might be where in order to enhance our understanding of memory, a researcher decides to look at those unusual cases where people with very low IQ tend to develop brilliant musical performance ability, or impressive factual knowledge in a specific area.

Structured samples

Structured samples fall into two main types: **strategic informant sampling** and **snowballing**.

- Strategic informant sampling is selecting the people whom you think can give you the most information. It may make more sense to seek information on social conditions in an area by asking community leaders, local doctors, social workers and community help and advice agencies than by sampling the population of the area itself. Such agencies collect, like magnets, this kind of information.

- Snowballing could be regarded as a kind of strategic informant sampling. The researcher asks a selected member of a population who else, he ought to ask to obtain useful information and then repeats the process with each of those he is told about. Thus, the number of informants snowballs.

Haphazard samples
A haphazard sample is merely one which is readily available. A teacher carrying out research on children may use his or her own class as subjects. Some of the most important early studies of memory resulted from a researcher (Ebbinghaus) sampling his own performance in memory tests.

HOW LARGE SHOULD A SAMPLE BE?

Key factors

This depends on a number of things:

1. Type of sample
The same level of precision can be achieved with a smaller sample if stratified random sampling is used, than is the case if pure random sampling is used.

2. Level of precision and confidence limits required
The tighter the precision levels and confidence limits you seek, the larger the sample you'll need.

3. Estimated findings (where percentage findings are sought)
The smaller the percentage occurrence expected, the larger the sample will need to be.

4. Variability of data
The more classifications you will be making in cross-tabulation, the larger your sample will need to be.

5. Time and costs constraints
Data collection is time-consuming and costly.

6. Size of working universe
The larger the working universe, the larger the sample needs to be.

SUMMARY

- Sampling is necessary for reasons of feasibility.
- Sampling can increase accuracy.
- We often need to sample from working universes.

- Sampling can be random or non-random.
- Random samples are good for predicting and explaining, while non-random samples are good for describing.
- There are various types of random and non-random sampling.
- What constitutes an appropriate sample size depends on a number of factors.

QUESTIONS AND ANSWERS

1. *If you are only taking a sample of the population, how can you be confident that it will give you a picture similar to that which you would get if you studied all the population?*

   Because of the law of regularity of large numbers, a sufficiently large sample will provide data which is representative of the population from which it is drawn. The larger the sample, the more representative it will be, although above 1,000 incremental advantages are minimal.

2. *It has been said that studying a sample can give you a more representative picture than studying all the population. This seems absurd.*

   No, its not absurd. The greater the number of cases dealt with the greater the number of data sets and the greater the number of processing errors possible.

3. *How can it ever be justifiable to use a haphazard sample?*

   When theory generation is the aim representativeness is not important. That is only important when you are testing the theory.

   Also, where small scale studies are involved, some attempt to randomise a sample is likely to introduce bias anyway. Suppose you were studying just twenty cases. If you sought to obtain these as a random sample of the UK population you would have cases dotted widely about the country containing the biases attached to the specific regions. To then claim the sample was representative would be misleading.

   In addition, the costs involved may become too great to be justified by the benefits; cost/benefit analysis is always relevant in research. The researcher must simply choose the best type of sample his budget permits, taking into account the costs of other aspects of his project and the relative benefits of a particular type of sample.

4. *How on earth do you choose between different kinds of random sample, or different kinds of purposive sample?*

   On the basis of both cost/benefit analysis and 'absolute cost', *ie* what the budget can stand.

   In addition, pure randomisation does not always produce the most representative results. Stratified random sampling, for example, may sometimes be best.

5. *What if there are people in a random sample whom you have reason to believe would deliberately, or unwittingly, distort the data? Suppose, for example, you were studying an organisation or a community and one of the people in the sample was likely to have a vested interest in the picture looking good. That person may be a manager, or owner in the case of an organisation, or a politician in the case of a community.*

   You would be justified in removing that person, or persons, from the sample, as long as you declared that you had done so and gave your reasons in your report. Users of the information could then make allowances for the omission. These are called mortality effects and will be dealt with in Chapter 7.

CASE STUDIES

George finds his working universe

George is interested in the relationship between family background and children's attitudes towards school. It would be difficult, if not impossible, to list every single child of school age in the country at the time of the study, but he has found a suitable working universe. There is a listing of everyone who was born during a particular week of 1972 (*The Child Health and Education Study*), for such people have been used in a large scale, on-going study.

George obtained the list of names and permission to send a questionnaire to a random sample of them. It is a rough rule of thumb that a sample should be as large as a researcher's time and cost budget allows, but little is ever gained in accuracy over 1,000 cases, so this was the sample size used.

Graham focuses on memory feats

Graham is interested in furthering our knowledge of memory. For some of his studies he focuses on people who have demonstrated outstanding memory feats (rare case sample) and seeks to explain why their performance is so different from most people's. By definition, rare cases are far and few between, so there's never the need to sample from them. Wherever a case is discovered, Graham seeks to study it.

Sylvia studies a women's refuge

Sylvia is interested in the outlooks of victims of violence. It would be impossible to establish a list of everyone who falls into this category, so she must be content with studying groups whom it is known have suffered in this way, *ie* working universes.

Sylvia has chosen to study women in a women's refuge. The refuge holds only a dozen or so women, so she will be able to include them all in her study. She chose a refuge which a friend introduced to her. This is as good a way as any when you are focusing on just one refuge. It involves bias, yes, because the nature and extent of violence suffered by women may vary from area to area, as may the way they, themselves, deal with it. Many things may influence this: levels of crime, alcoholism, unemployment and community norms, for example. But if Sylvia had closed her eyes and stuck a pin in a list of refuges the selection would have been no less biased.

DISCUSSION POINTS

1. Can you think of any groups which could be used as working universes of people with particular qualities? How closely would you guess they represent all people with those qualities?

2. Try to think of as many things as possible which may make the use of very large samples less accurate than small samples.

3. Have you ever been asked to take part in a survey? If so, what type of sample do you think was being used and why?

6
Analysing the Data

Having collected our data we now need to make sense of it. There are a number of basic statistical techniques which will make the data begin to mean something to us. If our purpose is merely description then those techniques may be all we need. However, if our intention is to go on and explain the data or predict from it, we will need to use more sophisticated techniques than these. This chapter should help you begin to get to grips with the techniques you need, whatever your aims.

STARTING SIMPLY

We begin with computing a number of **unidimensional** or, as they are sometimes called, **univariate statistics**. These are so named because they give information about one variable only; they do not tell us anything about how one variable is related to another. They are purely descriptive; they do not explain the data and do not, by themselves, enable us to make any predictions about it.

The frequency count

The first analysis we do is a **frequency count**. This gives us the frequency with which our data conforms to certain criteria. One example would be age groups of, say, 20-29, 30-39, 40-49, etc. It tends to be the first analysis carried out because other statistical techniques use it as a basis. An example of a frequency count is given in Table 1.

Age group	Frequency
20-29	941
30-39	1437
40-49	1289

Table 1. Example of a frequency count.

Averaging

It will also be useful for us to know the **arithmetic mean** of the data. Not only does this help to describe it, but this statistic is also used in subsequent, more sophisticated, statistical techniques. This is what most lay people think of as the average. It is all the values added together and then divided by the number of items. For example, the arithmetic mean of 18, 19, 22 and 23 = 82 (the total) divided by 4 (the number of values) = 20.5.

Misleading with averages

This can provide a useful way of evaluating the data, but it can also be very misleading. It may, in fact, be used to deliberately mislead, for example when a government, or a shadow cabinet, wants to make a bad situation seem good, or a good situation seem bad.

Consider the following highly simplified situation. Suppose a country has 20 million people, each with an income of £5,200 per annum, and 2 million people whose income was £52,000 per annum each. A government wishing to present a picture of affluence for the majority of the people could truthfully state that the average income of the population is £9,455 per annum. This gives a misleading picture as almost everyone is on not much more than half that figure.

Choosing the mode

The role of scientists, however, is to present the facts in the most meaningful way. For this situation a scientist would choose a different kind of average: the **mode**. The mode is the most frequently occurring value. In this case it would be £5,200 per annum, which is a much more useful statistic.

Choosing the median

There are situations where yet another kind of average may be appropriate: the **median**. This is the middle value of the range. It may be useful, for instance, to indicate that there were as many people under the age of 35 in the sample as there were above that age. The age 35, therefore, would be the median.

Knowing the range

It is also important to know the **range** of values in the data, because averages alone do not tell us enough to be able to meaningfully picture it. Suppose we have a mean IQ of 110 in a sample of 1,000 people. It could mean that all the sample members have IQs within 10 points of the mean, or could it mean that the sample contains IQ levels as low as 80 and as high as 170. We need to know the range, *ie* the lowest and highest values.

Standard deviation

Even if we know the range, the picture is still not very clear. There could be sizeable frequencies of IQ values all the way along the spectrum from the lowest to the highest levels. Alternatively, almost all the IQ values in the sample might cluster closely around the mean of 110. What we need to know is the **standard deviation**. This is a kind of average deviation from the mean, and with it we can develop a picture of the curve which describes the data. Scientific calculators can provide this statistic at the touch of a button.

Percentage tables

It may be useful to analyse the **percentages** of our sample which fall within particular classes. For example, it may be considered useful to list the percentages who are aged between 20 and 29, 30 and 39, 40 and 49, etc. An example of such a percentage table in given in Table 2.

Age group	Percentage of sample
20-29	25
30-39	40
40-49	35

Table 2. Example of a percentage table.

Analysing data over time

It may be that your goal is to analyse data over time, by means of trends, for example, as stock market analysts do. However, the ultimate goals of science are explanation and prediction. Most research, therefore, focuses on associations and relationships between two or more variables.

DEALING WITH TWO VARIABLES

Cross-tabulating

The simplest way of analysing for an association between two variables is to **cross-tabulate**. Cross-tabulation means presenting the values of one variable along the horizontal axis and the values of another on the vertical axis. An example is given in Table 3.

IQ class	Attainment score					
	40-49	50-59	60-69	70-79	80-89	Totals
90-99	100	20	0	0	0	120
100-109	20	90	80	10	0	200
110-119	10	80	260	80	20	450
120-129	3	67	50	20	10	150
130-139	0	1	9	20	50	80
Totals	133	258	399	130	80	1000

Table 3. Example of cross-tabulation of data.

Chi-square test

We need to know we are not being fooled by our data, that the associations being found are not merely due to chance. The technique for this where cross-tabulations are concerned is known as the **chi-square test**.

As was explained in the last chapter, if we want to test whether two variables are associated we formulate the hypothesis of the exact reverse, that is that they are not associated. If there is no statistical association between the variables of IQ and educational attainment scores, as presented in Table 3 above, then any found in the data would be a matter of chance. Based on chance alone we would expect each of the cells to contain a value of 40 (a sample of 1,000 divided by 25 cells) and this would support the null hypothesis, *ie* that the variables are not related. If, however, the matrix shows a different picture, as, indeed, it does in Table 3 above, it appears to challenge the null hypothesis, but before we accept the findings we carry out the following calculation.

Making the calculation

$$\chi^2 = \frac{\Sigma(O - E)^2}{E}$$

Where O = observed values and E = values expected on the basis of chance alone.

We then consult a table of degrees of freedom and locate the one appropriate for our calculation. The appropriate degree of freedom value is n-1, where n is the number of expected values in our matrix, *ie* the number of cells.

In the example provided in Table 3 above we have 25 cells. Therefore, in the table for degrees of freedom, we need to locate the entry against 24 degrees. Here it will provide **critical values** for 5 per cent and 1 per cent confidence levels that the observed findings are not due to chance, that is that no more than 5 in 100 or 1 in 100 could be expected to have this value by chance alone.

We must choose what level of confidence will satisfy us. If the result of our chi square test is higher than the critical values selected then we can reject the hypothesis that the findings are due to pure chance. At the same time we can accept that there is evidence of a statistical association between the variables we have been testing.

Coefficient of correlation

You don't have to cross-tabulate to test for an association between two variables; you can calculate a **coefficient of correlation** instead.

- A coefficient of correlation is a measurement of the degree to which the data conform to a **regression line** between one variable and the other.
- A regression line is a line of best fit between the plottings of one variable and another on a two-dimensional chart.
- Without the regression line this chart is called a **scattergram**.

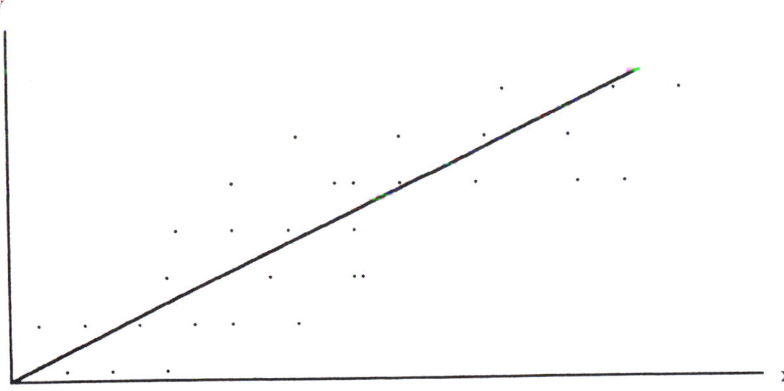

Fig. 8. Scattergram and regression line. (The purpose of this diagram is to show roughly what a regression line looks like. No accuracy is implied).

When you look at the plottings of one variable against another on a chart you will probably be able to judge roughly where the regression line will run. It is the straight line which most closely touches all of the plottings.

Scientists need to make more accurate judgements than common sense and a careful eye could provide, however. They plot the line in that position where the sum of the squares of the amounts by which it misses each of the plottings is lowest. This kind of regression line is called the **least squares regression line**.

It is also necessary to calculate how closely the plottings, in general, conform to the line. This will indicate how much of a change in one variable is associated with a change in the other.

Coefficient of determination

The **coefficient of determination** is a measure which can provide us with this information. The formula is as follows:

$$r^2 = \frac{\Sigma(\hat{Y} - \bar{Y})^2}{\Sigma(Y - \bar{Y})^2}$$

where $\hat{Y}$ = estimate and $\bar{Y}$ = mean

Pearson's product moment correlation coefficient

Scientists conventionally express the closeness of fit by means of a coefficient of correlation. Where values conform to at least an interval scale (where the intervals between one value and another are equal) the measure generally used is known as **Pearson's product moment correlation coefficient**.

The formula

$$r = \frac{S^2xy}{\sqrt{S^2_x \text{ x } S^2_y}}$$

where r = Pearson's product moment correlation coefficient, S^2_{xy} = the covariance of x and y and S^2_x = the variance of x and S^2_y = the variance of y.

The covariance of x and y is found by the following formula:

$$\frac{\Sigma XY}{n} - \frac{\Sigma X \bullet \Sigma Y}{n \bullet n}$$

The variance of x is found by the formula:

$$\frac{\Sigma X^2}{n} - \left(\frac{\Sigma X}{n}\right)^2$$

The variance of Y is found in the same way, substituting Y for X.

We now need to satisfy ourselves that the associations we have observed are not due to chance. For this we have to carry out a test of statistical significance. Again, we formulate the hypothesis that the results are due to chance and we set out to test it. If they are we would expect a zero correlation between X and Y if we tested the entire population. We begin by calculating a test statistic according to the following formula.

$$t = \frac{r - 0}{Sr}$$

where t = test statistic, r = correlation coefficient and Sr = standard error. The 0 represents the correlation which a test of the whole population would yield if these findings were entirely due to chance (it would not be zero otherwise).

To calculate the standard error the formula is:

$$Sr = \sqrt{\frac{1-r^2}{n-2}}$$

We then consult a table of degrees of freedom and select the one which is equal to the number of cases we are dealing with minus one. If our test statistic is greater than the critical values listed for 1 per cent confidence level or 5 per cent confidence level, as desired, we can be satisfied that the findings are not due to chance.

Spearman's rank correlation coefficient

Sometimes data does not even conform to at least an interval scale: there are not equal intervals between each value. Here we can use the **Spearman's rank correlation coefficient**. An example of this kind of data is data categorised by religion: Protestant, Catholic, Jewish, Muslim, etc. This kind of data is very different from, for example, IQ, where the differences between one score and the next – 100, 101, 102, etc – are equal.

Making use of correlation coefficients

It is not necessary to remember the formulae for these statistics as they are available at the touch of a button today, on scientific calculators and computers.

A perfect correlation has a coefficient of 1. The correlation coefficient indicates how much of the association between one variable and another is explained by the regression line. We cannot explain more than the whole, thus the coefficient correlation of 1. Nor can the line explain less than none of it, thus the minimum correlation coefficient value is zero. Correlation coefficients, therefore, can only lie between zero and 1. However, they can be positive or negative numbers, since just as one variable can increase as another increases, so it can decrease as the other increases. In the latter case the correlation coefficient would be negative and we would say there is an inverse correlation between the two variables.

Correlations below 0.7 are no good for prediction purposes, because here the variables have more differences than similarities. This is because the coefficient of determination r^2 is $0.7 \times 0.7 = 0.49$. The coefficient of determination tells us the proportion of a change in one variable which is tied up with a change in the other, *ie* the proportion of overlapping influences there are.

Level of significance

Only levels of 1 per cent and 5 per cent are used in measures of statistical significance. We call errors due to accepting findings which are really due to chance **type I errors**. The opposite case, errors due to wrongly assuming a finding is due to chance, we call **type II errors**. A level of statistical significance can, therefore, be thought of as the chance of making a type I error.

There is less chance of making a type I error if we only accept confidence levels of 1 per cent, than if we accept confidence levels of 5 per cent. Conversely, there is less chance of making a type II error if we accept confidence levels of 5 per cent.

Type I errors are the most important, since they could lead to erroneous findings being written up, published and naively used as foundations in subsequent research. Scientists have been aware of the dangers of extrapolation from erroneous theory since science began.

CONTROLLING FOR A THIRD VARIABLE

It may be that researchers have discerned an association between two variables, but they suspect that things are more complicated than they seem at first glance. Rather than a change in one causing a change in the other, they may suspect that a third variable is causing the change in each.

Such a situation is the explanation behind what are called **nonsense correlations**. An example of these is the fact that when the stork population increases so does the human birth rate. Clearly the stork population does not influence the human birth rate, but a **third variable** which influences both actually lies behind it. We call this an **intervening variable**.

The situation is not always so clearly nonsensical and so it is easy to assume that no third variable is involved.

- A third variable's influence can be tested by holding its value constant to see if the association between the other two still holds true. If it does, then it is not involved.

We call the one held constant the **test factor** and we refer to the act of holding a variable constant as **controlling** for that variable. It is also sometimes referred to as **partialling on** that variable. Clearly, such a test should only be carried out if there are reasonable grounds to believe the third variable may be involved. Otherwise we could end up testing everything in creation. This would be a waste of time and money. One way of controlling for a third variable is to produce two sets of cross-tabulations. In one the third variable is present while in the other it is not.

Conditional variables

A conditional variable conditions the relationship between X and Y, so that if it is removed, or held constant, the relationship changes.

Suppressor variables

Sometimes a third variable may suppress the influence of one variable on another. If it is removed the association between X and Y increases.

Antecedent variables

Although a change in X appears to cause a change in Y, the influence of X on Y may depend on a third variable T.

$$T \rightarrow X \rightarrow Y$$

DEALING WITH SEVERAL VARIABLES

It may be that a researcher wishes to explore the individual effects of components of a **frame variable**, *ie* its **dimensionality**.

- A frame variable is a variable which is, itself, made up of a number of variables, each contributing to its overall effect.

For example, family background is known to be responsible for about 40 per cent of a child's educational achievement. There is a whole host of influences in that frame variable of family background; the frame variable has a number of known dimensions. All of these make their contribution to the composite. The level of parental encouragement, for example, has been found to have the largest effect of all the family background factors. Things like the level of poverty, amount of space in the house and the availability of books and newspapers there also contribute to the overall effect, although to a less degree. We describe the unequal value of influences by saying they are **weighted**.

It is important to develop this kind of information. Otherwise attempts to replicate research may fail, simply because the mix of process variables in a frame variable tested is different.

Pre-requisite assumptions for dimensional analysis

There are a number of assumptions which have to be made before dimensional analysis can begin.

The first assumption

First, the independent variable and the dependent variable must be related in linear fashion. It is possible, however, to convert some non-linear lines to linear form for the purpose, using logarithms.

The second assumption

This is that the influences of the independent variables must be additive.

Example

x_i accounts for 20 per cent of effect
x_{ii} accounts for 10 per cent of effect
x_{iii} accounts for 60 per cent of effect
x_{iv} accounts for 10 per cent of effect

The third assumption

The third necessary assumption is that dimensional variables should correlate only slightly, if at all. An example might be: x_i correlating with x_{ii} 0.08, or x_{ii} correlating with x_{iii} 0.1.

Multiple regression or factor analysis techniques are used to measure the influence of each separate component of the composite independent variable on the dependent variable.

Making frame variables more useful

The more we understand the dimensions of a frame variable, the better we can develop its predictive value. The more dimensions are used in a battery of tests for the effect of a frame variable, the more accurately will be any prediction which is made from the study. By exploring the dimensional influences researchers are alerted to missing dimensions and can direct their efforts to discovering them.

If the component variables correlate highly with each other then they are not different dimensions but substantially the same thing. Their use will produce information which could mislead. The effects recorded for each dimension of the frame variable will not be additive for some part of the influences will have been recorded twice. This is why dimensions must correlate lowly with each other. Ideally, components should not correlate with each other at all; they should be pure dimensions. However, this is often just too much to expect of this kind of data.

Discovering causality

The ultimate goal of scientific research is to discover **causality**. **Path analysis** allows us to do this. Scientists tend to postulate that some kind of association will be found, based on a particular **theoretical model**.

- A theoretical model is a speculative construction of the way things relate to each other.

They then look to see if the data supports it. If it does not they modify the model and try again with new data.

A number of assumptions are necessary before path analysis can begin. They include all of those assumptions which it has already been stated are necessary for multiple regression, plus three others.

The first assumption

First, it is assumed that the causal order between the variables is known.

The second assumption

Secondly it is assumed that there are no influences from outside the system we envisage: we say the model is a **closed system**.

The third assumption

Thirdly, it has to be assumed that there is no reverse causality, *ie* when X influences Y the change in Y does not, in turn, make any further change in X. There are situations where this occurs; consider, for example, paranoia. A paranoid person gives behaviourial cues which make others think negatively about them. This, in turn, is perceived by the paranoid person and makes them even more paranoid. For path analysis the variables concerned must not be connected in this way. The postulated influence must flow in one direction only; we say it must be **recursive**, *ie* asymmetrical.

SUMMARY

- Start with simple, univariate statistical techniques: frequency count, averages, standard deviation, range and, perhaps, percentage tables.
- Associations between two variables can be investigated using cross-tabulation or correlation coefficients.
- Pearson's product moment correlation coefficient is appropriate for data which conforms to at least an interval scale.
- Spearman's rank correlation coefficient is appropriate for data which does not conform to at least an interval scale.
- Tests of statistical significance tell us how confident we can be that findings are not due to chance.
- Sometimes we need to test for the effect of a third variable.
- There are techniques for investigating several variables at once.

QUESTIONS AND ANSWERS

1. *If a statistical association is found does that mean that it is proven that one thing causes the other?*

   No. There can be reverse causality. Suppose a statistical association were found between parents' attitudes to their children's education, on the one hand, and the children's educational performance on the other hand. It could mean that the parents' attitudes partly caused the children's levels of achievement. However, it could also mean the children's school performance influenced the parents' attitudes to their education. If a child achieves highly parents may become enthusiastic about its education. If it achieves lowly they may lose interest.

   There could also be a third factor which causes changes in both variables. Statistical associations can also arise by chance (nonsense correlation).

3. *If, say, a 0.7 correlation is found between x and y and the direction of causality is established, does it mean that 70 per cent of y could be predicted from x?*

   No. You would have to take the square of that figure: $0.7^2 = 0.49$. This we call the coefficient of determination. We can say that 49 per cent of the variation in x can be predicted from a variation in y.

4. *What if you just have data, but don't have any knowledge of how it all fits together? What can you do?*

   There are techniques for finding factors in the data (factor analysis). These methods can reveal the dimensions of each factor found and also the ways the factors relate to each other. There are a number of such techniques, but they are beyond the scope of this book. If you wish to learn more about these you should consult a good statistics book.

CASE STUDIES

George uses Pearson's product moment correlation

George begins his analysis of data by computing a range of univariate statistics: frequencies, averages, standard deviation, etc. He checks his analyses carefully for key-punching errors and then carries out cross-tabulation, Pearson's product moment correlation coefficient and tests of statistical significance. It is 1 per cent levels of statistical significance which will influence policy makers most. There is less likelihood of acceptance of a false hypothesis at this level than there is at 5 per cent level.

Graham uses factor analysis

Graham uses factor analysis techniques to discover whether a single factor, two factors, or more factors are present in his data.

Sylvia compares, categorises and connects

Sylvia's analysis techniques are much less rigorous than George's or Graham's. They involve comparison and categorisation of data, careful definition of categories, identifying lines of connectivity (including causality) between them and hierarchical structuring.

DISCUSSION POINTS

1. Averages can be deceptive. Can you think of situations where it would be appropriate to use each of the following in the presentation of findings?

   - the mean
   - the median
   - the mode.

2. In what kinds of research data might it be useful to use percentage tables?

3. Do you know of any data where a third variable is responsible for what appears at first sight to be a perplexing association?

4. Can you think of situations where it might be more appropriate to accept only 5 per cent levels of confidence than 1 per cent levels?

5. Consider a piece of research which has been commissioned by educational policy makers. Do you think 1 per cent confidence levels should be required before policy changes are made based on the findings, or would 5 per cent confidence levels suffice? Give reasons for your answer.

7
Assessing the Quality of our Findings

When the data from a study has been analysed the quality needs to be critically appraised. We need to look carefully at the **reliability** and the **validity** and we need to test for a whole range of **alternative hypotheses**.

ASSESSING AND IMPROVING RELIABILITY

Reliability is the degree to which we could expect the same results if we or other researchers carried out the study again, using the same methods on another sample. Research methods vary in the degree of reliability they provide. Observation methods, particularly participant observation, are relatively unreliable, since the researcher's own subjectivity plays a significant part in the generation of data. By contrast, postal questionnaires are relatively reliable, because the participants do not come into contact with the researcher.

Testing for reliability

Perfect reliability is often beyond reach in social science but we must aim to achieve as high a level as possible. We can test the reliability of our findings in four ways.

The first method

First, we can carry out the study a second time on the same sample. The problem here, however, is that the participants' experience of being tested once already will, to some degree, affect their responses on the second testing. We have to assess how much this is likely to be the case. This method is called **test-retest reliability**.

The second method

A second way of testing reliability is to use different dimensions of the concepts we used the first time round. As a highly simplified example, suppose we tested intelligence using tests of verbal reasoning and abstract reasoning. We could, perhaps, retest using tests of perceptual speed, word fluency and short-term memory.

The problem with this method is that we need a good knowledge of the **dimensionality** of the concept we are using. **Dimensions** are components of a frame variable which each correlate highly with measures of that frame variable, but lowly with each other. Knowledge on the dimensions of a concept can be built up by studying all that is written on the subject. This method of testing for reliability is known as **multiple forms reliability**.

The third method

This is known as the **split half method**. Here we split the data categories randomly in half. In essence we are making two alternative forms of the test. For each respondent we then sum the values for each category in each half. This gives us an aggregate score for each half of the tests, for each participant. We then deduct the totals of one half from the totals of the other and calculate the mean difference. After this we calculate the variance of the differences. In the same way, we find the mean and variance for the total scores when the data is *not* split in half. The variance of the differences is then related to the variance of the unsplit scores in the formula:

$$r_{tt} = 1 - \frac{\sigma d^2}{\sigma T^2}$$

Where r_{tt} = split half reliability coefficient of the scale
σd = the variance of the differences between the scores on the two halves of the scale
σT = the variance of the total scores for the whole unsplit scale.

This gives us a reliability coefficient. Coefficients around 0.7 indicate moderate reliability, while those below 0.5 indicate that reliability is rather poor.

The fourth method

Fourthly, there is the **average intercorrelation method**. This requires the use of complex statistical computation and is beyond the scope of this book. The reader wishing to use this technique should consult a good statistics handbook. It is important that the items in the questionnaire being tested should be highly associated with each other.

Using a number of dimensions

The more dimensions of a concept used in a test, the higher the reliability can be expected to be. Ideally, we should aim to measure phenomena by using batteries of tests containing six or seven dimensions of the concepts we are measuring. No dimension is pure, otherwise it would not be a dimension, but the very essence of the concept. Therefore, when we measure them in order to measure a particular phenomenon we are measuring some irrelevant qualities too and this will bias the results. If we use a number of dimensions, biases in one direction can be expected to be compensated for by biases in another direction.

- It is random errors which negatively affect reliability
- Non-random errors affect validity. We will deal with this next.

ASSESSING AND IMPROVING VALIDITY

Suppose, in order to discover something about a particular population, we took a sample from it and studied it. We would need to satisfy ourselves that what we had tested was substantially what we had set out to test. In addition, we would need some assurance that the findings could be generalised to the population from which we sampled. In other words, we would need to assess:

- the validity of measures
- the validity of findings.

Achieving content validity

There are three ways we can seek to improve the validity of the findings we generate. First, we can use a number of dimensions of the concepts we are measuring, rather than using just one. As has already been pointed out, dimensions are never pure and to some degree are measuring irrelevant phenomena. By using more than one dimension the irrelevancies of one dimension may be compensated for by the irrelevancies of another. If this has been done to a high degree then the findings are said to have **content validity**.

Achieving criterion related validity

Another way is to test the degree to which the findings can predict the value of a target dependent variable.

Let's say, for example, a study has shown that social class is a powerful determinant of educational achievement. Suppose it has shown that the closer to the professional end of the spectrum a child's family lies the higher it can be expected to achieve. We could select a group of known underachievers whom we have not tested already and look to see if their social class backgrounds are as would be expected from our study. If we found they were, we could say our findings have **criterion related validity**.

Achieving construct validity

Yet another way of testing the validity of our findings is to consider the degree to which they confirm an existing theory. If they do we would say our findings have **construct validity**.

CHECKING FOR OTHER EXPLANATIONS

So out data appears to support our hypothesis, but are there other ways it could be explained? We call these other ways **rival hypotheses**. Various aspects of the testing process can be responsible for some or all of the effects observed and we need to examine these possibilities.

History effects

If testing takes place over a period of time the results may be affected by things, unconnected with the testing, which happened to the participants during the period of testing.

Suppose the effect of a curriculum change is being assessed by comparing the results in the end of year exams following the change with that found the year before the change was made. Any number of things outside the school could be, to some degree, responsible for any difference in the levels of achievement. Parents' concern for their children's future could have increased as a result of media stories of rising unemployment. Increases in ownership of computers at home could have made homework more tolerable. Perhaps a local club which had attracted teenagers to late-night concerts had closed down.

Maturation effects

Maturation effects are changes in the object of study as a result of the passage of time. Suppose we were measuring attitude change in a group of 14-16 year olds after they had received some kind of attitude modification therapy. It may be a mistake to attribute all of any change observed to the effects of the therapy. Some of the effects may simply be due to maturation, *ie* the children growing up.

Selection effects

Suppose we wanted to test the effectiveness of some form of behaviour modification therapy upon a sample of socially maladjusted children. We would have to acknowledge that the findings could not be generalised to all people, for this sample would be biased. The children's behaviourial problems would be more severe than others and so they may be more resistant to change. Alternatively, it may be that change would be more pronounced in this group than could be expected in others.

Instrumentation effects

Researchers are human beings. Some are more reliable and conscientious than others. They get tired, they get flu, they become increasingly familiar with the process and some may even get cocky and cut corners. An interviewer who is very tired or suffering from a heavy cold may not be as attentive as one who is fresh and in the best of health. The former may miss some important data which the latter will not.

Consider the street-corner market researcher who stops people and asks them a series of questions. In the midst of the traffic noise the researcher may not hear all the of the respondents' replies correctly. Also, after having conducted many interviews the researcher may have come to expect particular answers. Without realising it they might, by the way they ask the questions, lead respondents to provide the answers they expect.

Testing effects

When people are being tested they behave differently to when they are not. A classic example is when Elton Mayo and his team found that increasing the lighting in a factory resulted in an increase in productivity. Had the testing stopped there it might have been tempting to a naive researcher to attribute the increase in productivity to the increase in lighting. However, when the increase in lighting was removed productivity did not fall back to the original level. Some of the increase in productivity appeared, therefore, to be due to the fact that the workers were aware they were being studied.

Mortality effects

Sometimes part of the findings of a study can be attributed to important data having being lost due to some participants dropping out of the study.

Suppose the study sought to test whether asthma was on the increase or not. Let's say the study had taken readings at two points in time, with an interval of five years between them. Suppose its data showed there was no significant increase over that period. We must not be too hasty in concluding that asthma has not increased during that time. We must first look carefully at who has dropped out of the sample over the five years and, therefore, whose data is not included. What if they died of asthma?

Regression effects

We have to be particularly careful where a sample has been selected on the basis of an extreme level of some characteristic. If measurements have been taken at two points in time, part of the explanation for what is found can be expected to be the result of what are called **regression effects**.

Let's consider, again, the example given earlier, of testing a behaviour modification therapy on 14-16 year olds with severe social maladjustment. We would need to take this alternative hypothesis into account. If they are chosen for the sample at time 1 on the basis of an extreme social maladjustment score, we would expect them to have a score closer to the mean at time 2, regardless of any therapy.

Scientists have tried to explain this effect in a number of ways, including the fact that the more extreme the scores the greater the error involved.

Combinations of internal validity threats

The above threats to internal validity may at times combine.

Suppose, for example, we wish to test the effectiveness of two kinds of educational programme in terms of achievement levels. On the one hand we may have the liberal/progressive style of education, which seeks to tailor education to the needs of individual children. On the other we may have the traditional style which seeks to shape children to a fixed curriculum. Suppose we find the traditional method to be associated with the highest achievement levels, we must not be too hasty in attributing this all to the type of educational provision. Those in our traditional schooling sample may come from homes where conventional qualifications are valued more than in the homes of the liberal/progressive sample. Consequently, it would not be unreasonable to expect the latter group to spend less time on schoolwork, miss more days at school and leave school at an earlier age. Some of the difference may be attributable to this.

We would call this combination **differential selection/independent variable interaction**. The traditional schooling group would contain a disproportionate number of middle class children, and such children might be expected to receive more total hours of schooling than the liberal progressive group who may miss many hours because of absence and early leaving.

CHECKING WE ARE NOT LETTING OUR STATISTICS FOOL US

Sometimes part of the explanation for data comes from error due to statistical sources. An easy trap for the naive to fall into is the **fishing error rate**. Results which have been found to be statistically significant at 1 per cent or 5 per cent level sound very respectable. But suppose the study includes a whole array of results, say 100 or more. At 1 per cent level of confidence, one in a hundred can be attributed to chance alone and at 5 per cent level of confidence, 5 can.

CHECKING WHETHER OUR FINDINGS ARE SAMPLE BOUND

There are a number of alternative hypotheses which limit the generalisability of the findings to the general population. To the extent that the data suffers from this we say it is **sample bound**.

Reactive effects of data collection arrangements

To some degree the data generated may be attributed to the data collection arrangements. Participants in a study tend to 'psyche out' the researcher and may tell them what they think they want to hear.

Reactive effects of measures

When data has been collected at two points in time the first data collection session may have an influence on the data which participants provide in the second session. They will have had the chance to think about the kind of questions they are likely to be asked. They may even have practised answers they think will impress the researcher. They may be aware, from the previous session, of the kinds of responses which will bring forth a favourable reaction from the interviewer.

SUMMARY

- Evaluate the reliability of your findings.
- Evaluate the validity of your findings.
- There are ways of improving reliability of findings.
- There are ways of improving validity of findings.

- Explore all rival hypotheses.

QUESTIONS AND ANSWERS

1. *Do we really have to look for all possible rival hypotheses every time? It's a great deal of work.*

   Yes. Nobody promised research would be easy.

2. *Can't you choose your methods so as to cut down on this?*

   Yes. Experimentation is the least vulnerable to rival hypotheses, quasi-experimentation is arguably the most affected.

3. *Surely it is not always possible, or feasible, to build in tests of reliability. What can we do when this is the case?*

   You can triangulate by using a different method which has relatively high reliability.

CASE STUDIES

George must take several problems into account

George will carry out a split-half test on his data to assess the reliability. The method he is using provides a relatively high level of external validity, *ie* generalisability of findings to the general population. The level of internal validity, however, is relatively low, since subjects have to 'squeeze' their true responses into questionnaire categories which may not completely fit them. To a large degree the internal validity will depend on how well he has compiled his questionnaire.

It is inevitable that in George's survey different children will be seen at different times of the week and the year. It is possible that children interviewed on a Monday will express different attitudes to those interviewed on a Friday. This may be more due to the time of the week than to their salient attitudes to education.

There are other rival hypotheses to be dealt with too. What about those he is unable to reach, or who refuse to take part in the study? Would their data be significantly different from the rest? To what degree will the children be telling their interviewer what they think will impress him? Are there going to be some days when George and other interviewers in his team will be less alert in their interviewing than others? If so, will this affect the data? These are all questions which must be addressed in assessing the quality of the data in the study.

Graham considers history effects

Graham's main methodology is experimentation. This tends to offer relatively high reliability and high internal validity, though the external validity can be quite low.

There are rival hypotheses which need to be addressed in this work. If delayed recall is being tested after one week, could information to which the participants are exposed during that time distort their recollections to some degree? Furthermore, these history effects will not be the same for each of the participants; life treats everyone differently. There is no way of avoiding this, though, short of locking the subjects up in an empty room for the interval between testing sessions and this would neither be ethical nor completely foolproof.

Sylvia has special problems with reliability and validity

It is important for Sylvia to try to make her findings reliable. The kind of research she carries out poses special difficulties in this respect. Her analyses involve subjectivity on her part, and she must develop a sound understanding of how her own background and personality will lead her to interpret things in her own unique way. This she will have to declare in her report. She will have to describe the influences which are personal to her and which could be expected to have fashioned her interpretation. Any subsequent researcher who wishes to try to replicate her work can then try to make allowances for these influences, together with the inevitably different set of influences he or she will be subject to when comparing the two sets of findings.

In the same way, Sylvia must try to validate her findings as true representations of the outlooks of the people she is studying. Without attempting to do this, all she will have recorded is her own interpretation of those outlooks, which is not the same thing. She must try to strip away the influences on her own interpretation, layer by layer. She must also consider how her own social and political standpoints colour her interpretation, and make adjustments for this as if she had the social and political standpoints of the people she is studying. She must allow for the fact that her outlook, her values and beliefs, and her perceptual skills, have been changed by her training as a researcher and consider how much her interpretation would be different had this not been the case. And so the self analysis must go on. It's not easy. The goal is to arrive at the best attainable fit to the outlooks of the actual people she is studying.

Another way she can try to validate her findings is by presenting them to people themselves and asking them if she has got it right. This is not a foolproof method, though. For one thing the people may not be prepared to challenge the researcher's interpretation.

Sylvia admits she is sceptical about whether she can ever get close to producing a good representation of the outlooks of the people she studies. Even if her work does not amount to a good representation, however, she believes this is not the only criterion for judging its usefulness. It may be judged, she argues, on the basis of the degree to which it generates further research questions.

DISCUSSION POINTS

1. Think of as many as possible of the influences which could be expected to affect researchers' subjective interpretations of what they have seen.

2. To what extent do you think interview participants can be expected to tell researchers what they think they want, or expect, to hear? How much of a problem do you think this is? Have you ever done this?

3. Take any research findings with which you are familiar. Can you think of any rival hypotheses that could be applied? Have these been ruled out in the study?

8
Looking from Several Directions

WHY IS THIS NECESSARY?

Even in a physical world it is never possible to observe all the dimensions of an object from the same direction. A three-dimensional object cannot be fully understood without shifting the point of focus six times to observe its dimensions. Even then there may be nooks and crannies which are still obscured from view. As another example, consider a radio signal. It needs to be investigated from three angles before its source can be accurately determined. The same goes for all intangible objects of study.

- **Triangulation** is the application of different methods, theories, investigators, samples, conditions of occurrence and levels of analysis to the study of phenomena.

We triangulate to rule out alternative hypotheses, such as the phenomena observed being mere artefacts of the method used. It can also give some degree of confidence that the conclusions are not theory bound, or assumption bound, that any relationships concluded would not disappear if conditions were different, or that different observers would not perceive the same phenomena differently.

Triangulation prevents the development of theories which, though internally consistent, ignore alternative explanations. It can also reveal additional dimensions of concepts.

TYPES OF TRIANGULATION

The various types of triangulation which can be carried out are given below.

1. Triangulation of method

i. Within – method, *ie* replication.

ii. Between – methods, *ie* using different methods to study the same phenomena.

2. Triangulation of theory

Examining the findings from different theoretical standpoints to consider different interpretations.

3. Triangulation of investigator

Comparing findings where single observers have been used with those where several have been employed. This will increase confidence that investigator bias has not distorted the findings.

4. Triangulation of data

i. In terms of space, *eg* testing hypotheses in different geographical regions, or sub-cultures.

ii. In terms of time, *eg* testing hypotheses at different points in time.

5. Triangulation of analysis level

i. Whether aggregated data supports a finding produced by non-aggregated data, such as interview transcripts.

ii. Whether data from studies which focus upon interactions between members would reinforce, or challenge, findings which focus upon facts about individuals.

iii. Comparing data which represent facts, or something usefully comparable, as properties of groups to which the individuals belong. An example might be looking to see whether attitudes, elicited by questionnaires from local residents, towards the siting of a chemical waste disposal plant are consistent with the concerns expressed by the local residents' association.

UNDERSTANDING THE IMPORTANCE OF TRIANGULATION

Triangulation is crucial to research. Levels of commitment among researchers in the social sciences to this kind of research goal are, unfortunately, not as high as they should be. Researchers too often tend to be egocentric in their approaches, refusing to consider rival hypotheses, or take seriously the research of others.

The social-scientific community contains both purist and social-activist types of researcher. The latter have a commitment to social change and their research may be influenced not only by what they see, but also what they want to see. This, too, could help to explain the general lack of commitment to triangulation. The more politically charged areas of social science, thus, feature a variety of suspect conclusions and theories.

Using different data

It is all very well producing findings of increased public health using samples for the south west of England, but would they hold true if the same study was done on people living in central London, Tyneside or West Cumbria? Would the same findings be derived if they were based on tests carried out in the spring, as from tests carried out in the winter?

Using different data collectors

Data collectors may influence the data they generate to some degree and some methods are more prone to this problem than others. In interviews, for example, a researcher has a lot of power to influence the data they are generating. This comes in the form of a whole host of non-verbal cues which they can use and the variety of ways they can formulate and present their questions. Different interviewers have different personalities, different biases and different ways of looking at and making sense of the world. By using more than one data collector these errors will, to some degree, compensate for each other.

Using other methods

Methods act as filters revealing some kinds of facts but obscuring others. For example, questionnaires made up of closed-ended questions can provide highly comparable data, because they force the respondent to choose among a limited number of categories. Interviews can provide much finer detail, though less comparable. The data from a questionnaire survey may contain error due to the fact that respondents were forced to choose alternative options which were not truly appropriate. Such error may be revealed by triangulating with interview data.

As a second example, suppose a researcher is studying attitudes towards a new by-pass road. Analysis of interview transcripts may lead the investigator to infer that no discernable themes are present, the responses being too varied. However, a questionnaire survey may reveal a different picture. Here, the participants themselves may have been forced to say which themes their feelings were most closely aligned to.

Looking for other interpretations

What we see in a situation depends, to some degree, on our frame of reference. There are many ways of looking at the world and we cannot look from all the vantage points at once. Our frame of reference determines what we attend to, what we see as relevant or important, and the kinds of explanations that will satisfy us.

A behaviourist psychologist studying phobia behaviour, for example, would be interested only in the observable aspects. They would focus upon the overt behaviour and the things to which the person or animal being studied had previously been exposed. An explanation which links these two things in some way would satisfy them. A psychologist working in the psychoanalytical tradition would not focus upon these things and would not be satisfied with such an answer. Such a researcher would expect to find an explanation connected with the unconscious minds of the people studied.

SUMMARY

- We cannot begin to understand something until we have looked at it from several directions, or in several ways.
- Investigating in more than one way is known as triangulation.
- Triangulation can amount to using different data, methods, investigators, theories, times, places, or levels of analysis.

QUESTIONS AND ANSWERS

1. *You say there is lack of commitment to triangulation. Why is this?*

   The research community contains both purists (ivory towerists) and social activist type researchers. The former try to keep bias out of research and view their role as the pursuit of knowledge relatively divorced from considerations of what it will be used for. The latter type of researchers have missions of social change and this motivates their research pursuits. However much we may respect the motives and professionalism of those who fall into the latter category we cannot avoid acknowledging that triangulation may challenge findings they are happy with.

Another reason may be that trail-blazing for new facts is more exciting and, perhaps, more impressive to funding bodies than checking existing knowledge.

2. *How do you choose how to triangulate*?

   Assess the main weaknesses of your study and triangulate in a way which will compensate for them best.

   Example: If your study is based on experimentation, which has low external validity, perhaps you should consider triangulating with a survey, which has high external validity. Alternatively, if your sample was selected from a very biased working universe, try to choose a working universe which has different characteristics.

3. *Why is it so necessary to triangulate*?

   When science was still in its infancy Francis Bacon, founder of The Royal Society, pointed out that the advancement of scientific knowledge may be hindered by 'extrapolation from faulty theory'. Not only can erroneous findings mislead policymakers, but they can undermine the future development of knowledge, for other researchers may naively cite them as authority for assumptions on which they base their own research.

CASE STUDIES

George has built-in interviewer triangulation

It would not be unreasonable to suspect George's findings of being sample bound. His sample members were all the same age when he surveyed them. Attitudes towards school can be expected to change throughout children's school lives. One way of taking account of this would be to triangulate the study with a random sample of older or younger children.

The findings could also be method bound due to the children telling the researcher what they think will impress him. This could, perhaps. be offset by comparing levels of extra-curricular activity, or truancy levels, with the home background index used in the study.

George's method – questionnaires completed by interviewers – is not particularly prone to investigator bias. It is not out of the question, though, since his questionnaire contains some open-ended questions. George's sample is large, however, and he has not envisaged seeing all the participants himself; he is using a small team of research assistants. Some degree of interviewer triangulation, is, thus, built into this design.

Graham's findings could be sample bound

Graham is using a working universe and it is remotely possible that his findings could be sample bound. The members of his working universe are all aware that they have a high IQ and have joined a society exclusive to those with high IQ. Their level of confidence in, and motivation to use and demonstrate their ability, may be higher than would be found in the general population of people of similar IQ. It is possible that this may, to some degree, influence their performance in the tests concerned.

The data could, perhaps, be triangulated by using a different working universe. He could, for example, select those who score in the 99th percentile in a series of school-year wide studies carried out in randomly selected parts of the country.

Sylvia's findings could be method bound

Sylvia is the first to admit her findings may be method bound. The very interaction of the researcher with the people she is studying will produce a kind of distorting subjectivity. This is over and above that which would affect either the people's own interpretation of their experiences, or the researcher's interpretation of what they say.

This may be overcome by triangulating with discourse analysis methodology, or studying tapes, written accounts, letters, or whatever. No face-to-face contact need be made here, so that distorting level of subjectivity will not arise.

DISCUSSION POINTS

1. How and why might the same situation studied by two different researchers produce different findings? Do you know any examples in the literature? Can you think of hypothetical examples?

2. How might you expect findings to differ between self-report data on memory quality collected by questionnaire and data collected by experimentation?

3. Would there be any point in testing people on an intellectual task at more than one time of the day?

4. Could there be any justification to testing them at different locations, such as in the laboratory and at home?

9
Reporting Research

When we have finished our research project we have to write up the report.

GROUNDING IN THE LITERATURE

Scientific enquiry is purposeful; its aim is to increasingly fill in the gaps in published knowledge. Consequently, it is important when presenting the findings to show where they fit into the already established knowledge. Furthermore, understanding the findings may require foundational knowledge which all readers may not have, or may have, but need reminding of. We need, therefore, to provide an adequate coverage of the background to the study.

FOCUSING OUR REPORT

Since our purpose is to fill a gap in the knowledge it is necessary to illuminate exactly where that gap lay before the present study was completed. Since knowledge is always complex and multi-layered, especially in social science, this task may need considerable care. It is also useful to say how important it was to bridge this gap and what it will do to advance the course of science. At this stage researchers may also define their parameters, *ie* the limits of their research. They might, for example, state what the project was *not* looking for.

DESCRIBING OUR METHOD

It is important to describe our methodology concisely, but comprehensively enough to facilitate replication. Readers must be given sufficient information about the method used to enable them to completely replicate the study on another sample if desired. The question to ask in deciding whether to include some detail or other is: Is it necessary for anyone who wishes to replicate the study?

It is also useful to provide a brief history of the development of the methodology used, partly to justify its use.

FINDINGS

The findings of the study should be presented concisely but comprehensively. Quantitative data should be presented in tabular and graphic form, using such things as graphs, bar charts and pie charts.

EXPLAINING CONTRIBUTION TO KNOWLEDGE

The findings of the study should be fully discussed in a section of its own. In this section the quality of the findings should be criticised, including their reliability and validity. Alternative explanations should be declared (see Chapter 7).

Consider how much of a contribution the findings make to the present state of knowledge and how important this contribution is. The implications for future research need to be considered, as do the implications for already published findings. The present study's findings may throw considerable doubt on, or undermine, current knowledge for example. Alternatively, the findings may have overcome an obstacle and cleared the way for a whole host of new lines of enquiry. The researcher may, in fact, suggest future directions of research based on the findings of the present study.

WRITING UP

The classical style of writing a research report is:

- contents list
- list of illustrations
- acknowledgements
- abstract
- introduction
- review of the literature
- focused review of the literature
- method
- findings
- discussion
- summary
- conclusions
- bibliography
- appendices.

The abstract
The abstract is a one-page précis of the research project: what it found, how it found it, how it selected its sample and the contribution it makes to knowledge.

The discussion section
The discussion section contains the criticism and the quality of the data referred to in Chapter 7.

The bibliography
The bibliography provides the full references of all the works referred to in the study. It is important as it enables readers to check references made in the text.

The appendices
The appendices are copies of all the instruments used in the study, *eg* questionnaires, coding instructions, and so on.

Being clear
Use plain English as much as possible when writing up the report. Explain all abstract terms used and avoid ambiguity. Standard research reporting guidelines are contained in Government Publication BS4811. Guidance on referencing and citation can be found in BS1629. BS7581 provides standards for graphs and tables. Alternatively, the research may follow the international standards contained in ISO 690. These should all be available at the university library.

SUMMARY

- Begin with a literature review.
- Identify the gap in the knowledge which the results fill.
- Describe your method.
- Present your findings.
- Discuss your findings.
- Explain their contribution to knowledge.
- Provide an abstract.

- Provide all the appropriate preliminary matter.
- Provide all the appropriate endmatter.
- Use plain English.

QUESTIONS AND ANSWERS

1. *Is this the only way to write research reports? Is there no variation in style?*

   Yes. There are some conventional differences between disciplines. The way to ensure you are meeting the standard of your discipline is to adopt the style used in your professional society's journal.

2. *Why is it necessary to be so pedantic about style of report writing? Surely it's the substance that matters.*

   Yes, but there has to be some standard, otherwise things would atrophy to unacceptable levels. Furthermore, just try getting published if you don't get your style right. What is the point of developing knowledge if you can't get it published?

3. *How do you decide which documents to include in your report appendices?*

   You have to include all the documents which would be necessary for someone to replicate your work.

DISCUSSION POINTS

1. Would you begin your research by thoroughly reviewing the literature, including writing up your review? Would you substantially leave the task of writing up the review until the whole project was finished? Would you consider this an on-going task throughout the research project? Justify whichever your answer is.

2. How much detail do you think you should give about your method?

3. Would you write up as you go along, or leave it until you have carried out your tests and analysed your findings? Why would you do things this way?

10
Being Ethical

There are a number of ethical issues which have to be understood in relation to research.

PROTECTING PARTICIPANTS

If a researcher is experimenting to discover the effect of something on humans, he obviously does not already know what that effect will be. Exposing the participants to whatever it is, therefore, puts them at some risk. There have been some horrifying instances of callous disregard for human welfare in the name of science.

The foundations of much of behaviourist psychology can be routed back to a study where a nine-month old child was made to fear rabbits, dogs, monkeys, cotton wool, a fur coat and other things. This was to test whether Pavlov's classical conditioning findings relating to dogs could be generalised to humans. The baby was conditioned by presenting a white rat in front of it at the same time as a frightening noise was made behind it, once a week for seven weeks. The infant came to associate the white rat with fear and this conditioned response became spontaneously transferred to the other items: the rabbit, the dog, the cotton wool, etc.

Many other horrifying incidents have and, undoubtedly, still do take place in the name of science. Few would disagree that scientists should not involve themselves in such practices. Not only that, but they should consider carefully the risk to the welfare of participants of any experiments they are encouraged to take part in.

Obtaining consent

Where there is some risk, and of course this is often the case, participants should be asked for their **informed consent**. This is a different thing from uniformed consent.

- Informed consent means that researchers have satisfied themselves

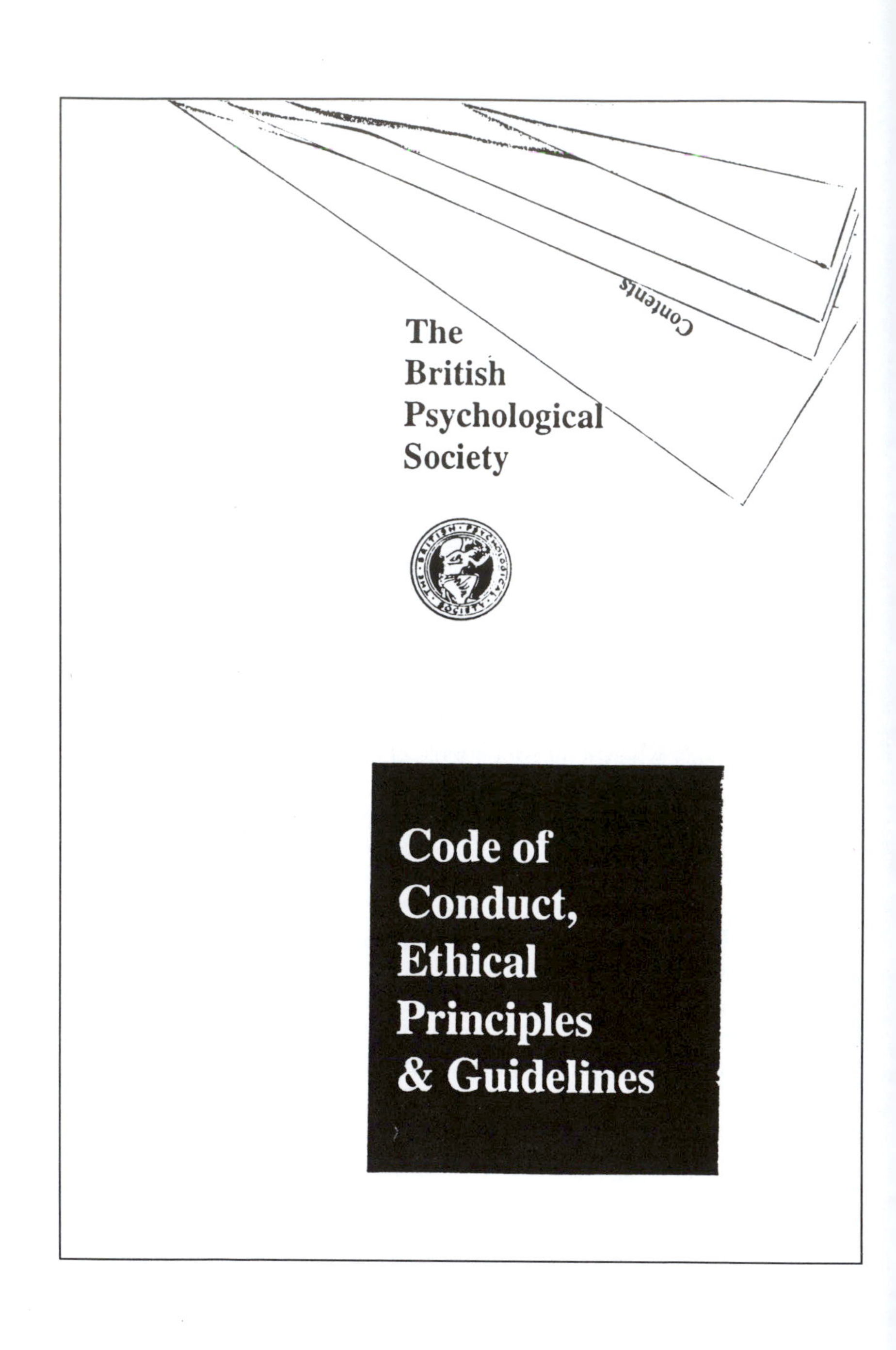

Fig. 9. Published Code of Conduct for members of The British Psychological Society.

that the participants had an adequate understanding of the risks they would incur, before they gave their consent.

The term 'adequate' understanding is used here because full understanding will be unattainable. The findings of the project are necessary before we can approach that level of understanding.

It is also important to inform participants that they are free to terminate their involvement in the research at any time.

ENSURING CONFIDENTIALITY

First, data obtained from participants should be treated with the utmost confidentiality.

Secondly, any data stored must comply with the Data Protection Act.

MAKING OUR WORK REPLICABLE

Replication is important to science. Only this way can we ensure that findings are reliable. It is incumbent upon researchers, therefore, to do all they can to facilitate replication of their work by others. This requires full disclosure of the methodology used.

Presenting findings in prosaic language, rather than in quantitative form, can hinder replication. The use of ambiguous language also makes the process difficult.

UNETHICAL USE OF FINDINGS

Researchers should be aware that science is not ethically neutral. Science produces knowledge and knowledge gives power to the beholder. Just as scientists' work may be used by some for socially desirable purposes, so it may be used by others for undesirable ones.

SEEKING GUIDANCE ON ETHICS

Scientists are not expected to be expert moral philosophers. Where they experience a moral dilemma in the practice of their research they should seek guidance. Professional associations tend to have established codes of conduct. The British Psychological Society, for example, publishes a booklet of 45 pages for this purpose (see Fig 9). Researchers should consult the code of conduct of their professional association and if they are still in doubt about the ethics of an aspect of their work they should discuss it with the appropriate officer of the society. Another way of clarifying ethical issues is by discussion with peers.

OTHER ETHICAL MATTERS

- The contributions of all the people who collaborated and assisted with a project should be fully acknowledged.
- Respect for intellectual property should also be maintained, and any knowledge drawn upon in producing the report should be attributed to those by whom it was first discovered.
- The sources of funding of a research project should also be disclosed.

SUMMARY

- Take care to protect the interests of participants.
- Treat personal information as confidential.
- Make your work replicable.
- Acknowledge all collaboration in and contributions to the project.
- Avoid association with unethical research.
- Seek guidance on ethics where necessary.

QUESTIONS AND ANSWERS

1. *You imply that scientists should put values aside, yet you also say they should be aware that science is not value free. Surely these two pieces of advice are contradictory.*

   Yes. The answer is not clear cut. It's a dilemma and it's you, as a researcher, who must handle it. It would be wrong for me to demand exactly how you do that.

2. *You say that attention must be given to protecting participants, but surely the law gives that protection. It would be against the law to put them at risk.*

   You'd be surprised. There are numerous cases of research subjects' interests being gravely infringed and their health put at serious risk.

3. *You could change the names of participants, but you could never*

guarantee to conceal their identities. Other characteristics mentioned in the report could identify them.

Yes, that's true. Again, it's not foolproof. All you can do is try your best to disguise them. One way to disguise names is to pick names our of the local telephone directory. You could just divide up the telephone book by the number of names, *ie* if there are five hundred pages and twenty-five names used you could take every first name on every twentieth page.

4. *What if a subject is willing to be named in the report?*

   It's another dilemma. The problem is that identifying one person by name could give clues to the identity of others in the sample, who do not want to be named.

CASE STUDIES

George ensures confidentiality

Not all the personal data George uses is completely under his control. Some of it is stored in the main database. He neither had any involvement in generating this, nor has he any influence over the confidentiality with which it is treated, except for where it has been extracted and used in his own studies. Access to this data base is, however, restricted to *bona fide* researchers.

As for the data George collects himself, however, he takes great care to keep it secure and treat it in strictest confidence. He publishes mainly statistical facts derived from it. He does use cases to illustrate findings, though. When this is so, he ensures that names are changed.

Graham clarifies ethical issues

Graham is a member of The British Psychological Society, which publishes a members' code of conduct. He finds this usefully clarifies the ethical issues in his work and he makes sure he abides by this code.

He encounters no glaring ethical dilemmas in his work. Testing memories is unlikely to put any of his subjects at risk of harm. Confidentiality of records has to be maintained, however. The methodology used lends itself well to replication.

Sylvia faces a dilemma

Sylvia comes up against ethical problems more than George or Graham. She takes great care to protect the identity of her subjects. She treats all information in strictest confidence and changes all names to conceal the identities of those from whom she collects data. The trouble is that it is still possible that they could be recognised in the published report. This poses a dilemma.

Another dilemma is posed by the fact that she may be told information in confidence regarding unlawful acts.

As has already been said, it is difficult to make Sylvia's work replicable. She does acknowledge the problem, though, and tries to be as open and declaratory as possible about the influences which will have shaped her interpretations.

Sylvia acknowledges all collaboration and contributions to her project, but she does not, of course, disclose the identities of those who provided data. She is always ready to seek guidance with ethical questions.

DISCUSSION POINTS

1. What would you regard as unethical research?

2. Is it ever justifiable to study people for a research project without disclosing to them that you are doing so? If so, *when* is it justifiable and when not?

3. Can you foresee any grey areas where you would feel you would have to seek guidance on ethics?

4. There are many instances in the literature where the interests of participants in experiments have not been adequately protected. Can you think of any?

Glossary

Abstract. A one-page précis of the research project: what it found, how it found it, how it selected its sample and the contribution it makes to knowledge.

Alternative hypothesis. See **rival hypothesis.**

Antedecent variable. A third variable on which an association between two other variables depends.

Arithmetic mean. All values added together and then divided by the number of items.

Closed-ended questions. Questions which permit only a limited range of answers. They may be of binary choice type, *eg* permitting yes/no, or multiple choice type, *eg* strongly agree/agree/indifferent/disagree/strongly disagree.

Coefficient or correlation. A statistic which indicates how much of the association between one variable and another is explained by the regression line. We cannot explain more than the whole, thus the maximum coefficient of correlation is 1. Nor can the line explain less than none of it, thus the minimum coefficient of correlation value is zero.

Coefficient of determination. A statistic which indicates the proportion of overlapping influences between two variables.

Conditional variables. A conditional variable conditions the relationship between x and y, so that if it is removed, or held constant, the relationship changes.

Construct validity. The degree to which a finding confirms an existing theory.

Content validity. The degree to which the different dimensions of a concept have been included in the overall measurement of the concept, thus compensating for irrelevant measures.

Control group. A sample which is tested alongside a target group, but unlike the target group is not exposed to the independent variable. The differences in findings between the two groups can, therefore, be attributed to the effect of the independent variable.

Covert research. Research carried out on people, or groups, without their knowledge.

Cross-tabulation. Tabulating one set of data against another in rows and columns, *eg* age groups plotted against conservativism scores.

Ex-post facto research design. *Ex-post facto* means after the fact. Such a research design therefore attempts to discover knowledge from events in the past. This is unlike most social research, which focuses on studying behaviour occurring in the present.

External validity. The degree to which findings from a sample can be generalised to the general population.

Fishing error rate. Even at 1 per cent level of statistical significance, one in a hundred findings can be expected to be due to chance. This is known as the fishing error rate.

Frequency count. A tabulation of the frequencies with which each value of a variable is found in a set of data.

General universe. The entire population of people or things in which the researcher is interested and from which he/she has, by one means or another, drawn a sample for testing.

Generalisability. See **external validity**.

Grounded theory. Theory developed inductively from data, rather than by hypothesis testing.

Haphazard sample. One which is merely readily available. A teacher carrying out research on children may use his or her own class as subjects, for example.

History effects. If testing takes place over a period of time the results may be affected by things unconnected with the testing, which happen to the participants during the period of testing. These are known as history effects.

Hypothesis. A postulated connection between two or more variables for the purpose of testing. Scientists formulate at least two hypotheses each time they wish to test for an association between two variables. These are known as a target hypothesis (H_1) and a null hypothesis (H_0). The first says the data will show evidence that a suspected association exists, the second says it will not. It is the latter hypothesis which is tested.

Independent variable. A variable being tested as a cause of a change in another variable (dependent variable).

Instrumentation effects. Effects which are due to some aspect of the researcher rather than to the independent variable, *eg* inaccurate measurement due to tiredness.

Internal validity. The degree to which methods have been measuring what the researcher set out to measure.

Interscorer reliability coefficient. A measure of the consistency with which two or more analysts assess or score data. The analysts may, for example, be observing behaviour, or interpreting interview transcripts. If fewer than half the measurements are comparable then interscorer reliability is certainly low and the findings suspect.

Interval scaling. Where the differences between the rankings of data can be quantified, but there is no absolute zero point. IQ is one such variable.

Interview schedule. A schedule of themes to serve as a guide for conducting interviews.

Least squares regression. A line drawn through plottings on a scattergram in such a position that the sum of the squares of the amounts by which it misses each of the plottings is lowest.

Longitudinal study. A research design for studying behaviour on an ongoing basis. This contrasts with snapshot-type studies which focus on behaviour at one point in time only. An example of a longitudinal study is the Child Health and Education Study, which aims to observe a large sample of people throughout their entire lives.

Maturation effects. Maturation effects are changes in objects of study as a result of the passage of time.

Median. The middle value in a range.

Mode. The most frequently occurring value in a set of data.

Model. A conceptualisation of the way two or more concepts relate to each other. Models can be of descriptive or explanatory type. They can also be normative or heuristic. The former makes a statement about how things ought to be or normally are. The latter is designed to aid exploration of the phenomena concerned.

Mortality effects. When part of the findings of a study can be attributed to important data having been lost due to some participants dropping out of a study.

Multiple regression. A statistical technique used to measure the influence of each separate component of the composite independent variable on the dependent variable.

Null hypothesis. When scientists wish to find out whether two things are related they formulate a statement that they are – a **hypothesis**. It is conventional for scientists to state two hypotheses: the **target hypothesis** (H_1) and a null hypothesis (H_0). A null hypothesis simply states that the relationship will not be found.

Open-ended questions. A question which does not limit the answer to yes, no or a range of set alternatives, *eg* red, green or yellow. Participants can answer the question any way they like.

Ordinal scaling. If a variable has ordinal scalar properties it means the data can be ranked, although no precise calibration can be applied, *ie* the differences between the ranks cannot be quantified. Differences in people's power and authority, as represented on a company structure chart, take this form.

Participant observation. A research design where the researcher joins the group being studied as an active member, in order to be able to interpret the data through the group members' frame of reference.

Phenomenological validation. The researchers declare all the influences in their biographies which may have affected their interpretation of the data. Their age, sex, social class, political affiliations, personal experiences and even their scientific paradigm can all be expected to be influences. Such declaration enables readers and users of their findings to take these influences on interpretation into account.

Post-testing. Testing samples after exposure to an independent variable.

Pre-testing. Testing samples prior to exposure to an independent variable.

Purposive sample. Any sample selected in a non-random fashion. Here the chance of any member of the general population being selected is either nil, 100 per cent or unknown.

Random sample. Where every element has an equal chance of being chosen.

Ratio scale. Scaling of data where not only are the calibrations between the rankings precisely quantifiable, but the scale also has an absolute zero point. Scaling of temperature is an example.

Regression effects. Where a sample has been selected on the basis of some extreme level of some characteristic, and measures are taken at two points in time, part of any difference can be explained in terms of the tendency data has to regress towards the mean.

Reliability. The degree to which we could expect the same results if we or other researchers carried out the study again, using the same methods on a similar sample.

Replication. Repeating a study on a similar sample to establish whether the same results would be found.

Retrospective interviewing. Interviewing people to gain information on past events and conditions.

Rival hypothesis. A way of explaining data besides the target hypothesis.

Selection effects. Effects of sample bias on the dependent variable.

Snowballing. A sample compiled by starting with a small group and asking the members for referrals to others who may also be prepared to participate.

Strategic informant sampling. A sampling method designed to capitalise on the fact that knowledge is unequally distributed. Community leaders may, for example, be selected to supply knowledge regarding the overall situation in a community. Others without such rank may be selected to supply more detailed knowledge.

Stratified random sampling. Dividing the working universe up according to relevant characteristics, such as age, sex, occupational group. Random samples are then selected from each section.

Suppressor variable. A third variable which suppresses the effect of one variable on another.

Systematic sampling. A method of selecting a sample wherein every nth number is selected, *eg* every 10th house.

Target group. The group which is exposed to the independent variable, by contrast with the control group which is not exposed.

Target hypothesis. A statement of a proposition which a researcher suspects the data will support.

Test retest reliability. An assessment of reliability based on a retest of the same group to see if the results are similar to the first testing.

Testing effects. A source of spuriousness in findings due to the effects of being tested. People behave differently when they know they are being observed.

Theoretical construct. A statement supported by evidence that two concepts are related in some way. Do not confuse this with a theory; that requires two or more interrelated constructs.

Triangulation. The application of different methods, theories, investigators, samples, conditions of occurrence or levels of analysis to the study of phenomena.

Validity. The degree to which the study has measured what it set out to measure.

Variable. A concept which can differ in its essence. The sex of a person is a variable since it can take one of two forms, male or female. The content of some variables tends to differ in measurable degrees, so we call them quantitative variables. Age is one example of the latter.

Working universe. A known cluster of people, or things, with the qualities in which a research project is interested.

Further Reading

American Psychological Association (1987) *Casebook of ethical principles of psychologists*. WASHINGTON: American Psychological Association.

British Psychological Society (1993) *Code of conduct, ethical principles and guidelines*. LEICESTER: British Psychological Society.

Burgess, R. G. (ed.) (1984) *The research process in educational settings*, LONDON: Faber.

Cook, T. D. and Campbell, T. T. (1979) *Quasi-experimentation: design and analysis issues for field settings*. BOSTON: Houghton Mifflin.

Ely, M. et al. (1991) *Doing qualitative research: circles within circles*. LONDON: Falmer.

Glaser, B. G. and Strauss, A. G. (1967) *The discovery of grounded theory*. CHICAGO: Aldine.

Harris, P. (1986) *Designing and reporting experiments*. MILTON KEYNES: Open University Press.

Henry, G. T. (1990) *Practical sampling*. NEWBURY PARK, CA.: Sage.

Huff, D. (1994) *How to lie with statistics*. NY: Norton.

Jorgensen, D. (1989) *Participant observation: a methodology for human studies*. BEVERLY HILLS, CA.: Sage.

Kendall, M. G. (1962) *Rank correlation methods*. 3rd. edn. LONDON: Charles Griffen.

Kimble, G. R. (1978) *How to use (and misuse) statistics*. ENGLEWOOD CLIFFS, NJ: Prentice Hall.

McCall, S. and Simmons, J. (1969) *Issues in participant observation*. READING, MA.: Maddison Westley.

Mishler, E. (1986) *Research interviewing*. HARVARD: Harvard University Press.

Owen, F. and Jones, R. (1994) *Statistics*. 4th edn. LONDON: Pitman.

Slonim, M. J. (1960) *Sampling*. NY: Simon and Schuster.

Valentine, E. (1992) *Conceptual issues in psychology*, 2nd Edn. LONDON: Routledge.

Watford, G. (ed.) (1991) *Doing education research*. LONDON: Routledge.

Index

CRITICAL THINKING FOR STUDENTS

How to use your recommended texts on a university or college course

Roy van den Brink-Budgen

Interest in the role of Critical Thinking in education has increased enormously over the past ten years. This handbook provides a straightforward introduction to the subject, showing A-Level and university students how to recognise and evaluate the arguments they will meet in their studies. By making them better critical thinkers, it will help them not only to understand their course material but also to produce better essays and reports. Roy van den Brink-Budgen PhD has developed materials in Critical Thinking for a major school examination board.

96pp illus. 1 85703 400 7.

HOW TO STUDY ABROAD

Your guide to successful planning and decision making

Teresa Tinsley

Studying abroad can open up a whole new horizon of opportunities, but what courses are available? How does one qualify? What does it cost? Can anyone do it? Now in a fully updated third edition, this book brings together a wealth of fascinating advice and reference information. It covers what to study (everything from short study visits to postgraduate opportunities), getting a place, entrance requirements, when and how to apply, grants and scholarships, helpful agencies and contacts, validation of courses, what to expect (teaching, services), financing your stay, accommodation, fitting in, travel and visas, health and insurance and more, and complete with a country-by-country guide. 'The book is straightforward to use, with a good index, lists all the main reference sources likely to be found in a careers library, and is just the thing to provide a quick answer to those difficult questions.' *Phoenix/Association of Graduate Careers Advisory Services*. Teresa Tinsley BA DipEd MIL is Conferences Organiser at CILT, the Centre for Information on Language Teaching.

176pp illus. 1 85703 169 5. 3rd edition.

HOW TO STUDY & LEARN
Your practical guide to effective study skills

Peter Marshall

Are you thinking of studying or training for an important qualification? Do you know the right techniques for studying and learning, to ensure you achieve the best results as quickly as possible? Whether you are at college or university, doing projects and assignments, writing essays, receiving continuous assessment or preparing for exams, this is the book for you. In practical steps it covers getting your thinking right, organising yourself properly, finding and processing the information you need, reading effectively, developing good writing skills, thinking creatively, motivating yourself, and more. Whatever your subject, age or background, start now – and turn yourself into a winning candidate. Dr Marshall has a wealth of experience as a university and college teacher.

160pp illus. 1 85703 062 1.

STUDYING AT UNIVERSITY
How to make a success of your academic course

Kevin Bucknall

University life is wonderful and exciting but many students at first find it mysterious and a little frightening. It can be hard to adjust to the high degree of academic freedom. This book will help to banish any fears by explaining how to adapt to the pressures of your new course. You will learn what is expected of you and how to meet these demands week by week. The skills you need are best learned early in your first year but they will be constantly used during the whole of your time at university. These skills include taking notes, finding information, and then using it effectively in essays, orals and exams. Dr Kevin Bucknall has over 30 years' experience in university teaching in England and Australia. He presently teaches economics to first year students.

160pp illus. 1 85703 219 5.

HOW TO WRITE AN ASSIGNMENT
Improving your research and presentation skills

Pauline Smith

Assignments play a large and increasingly valuable role in studying and learning in further and higher education. Written by an experienced tutor/lecturer, this book offers the student a clear framework for his or her own assignment-based work, and encouraging the development of such skills as information gathering, evidence evaluation, argument and presentation, which will prove valuable not only on educational courses, but in the wider workplace beyond. An experienced teacher, chief examiner and Open University tutor, Pauline Smith now lectures at Manchester Metropolitan University.

108pp illus. 1 85703 210 1. 2nd edition.

HOW TO WRITE YOUR DISSERTATION
A practical survival guide for students

Derek Swetnam

Almost all advanced educational courses now include a dissertation or research project of some type. For many students this can be a terrifying experience as the time for submission approaches and tutors are elusive. Although colleges and universities may have different systems, basic principles for planning research and making the inevitable compromise between what is desirable and what is feasible are the same. Some mature students may not have written extensively for years but it is assumed that they can cope with minimum help. This new book offers a plain guide to ways of producing an excellent dissertation with minimum stress and frustration. It covers choosing a subject, planning the total work, selecting research methods and techniques, written style and presentation. The author is a former Course Leader of a large Master's level programme at the Manchester Metropolitan University.

102pp illus. 1 85703 164 4.

STUDYING FOR A DEGREE
How to succeed as a mature student in higher education

Stephen Wade

If you are an aspiring student in adult education, or a mature learner looking for a higher education course leading to a degree, this book is specially for you. It will lead you through the academic maze of entry procedures, study programmes and teaching methods. It explains how to apply and how to contact the professionals who will help; how to survive tutorials, seminars and presentations, and how to manage your time, plan your study, and find the right support when you need it. There are sections on the credit award system, pathway planning, and useful case studies of typical students in this context. Stephen Wade PhD has 20 years' professional experience in further and higher education, and is a Course Leader for a degree programme.

128pp illus. 1 85703 415 5.

GOING TO UNIVERSITY
How to prepare yourself for all aspects of student life

Dennis Farrington

Are you an A-Level student? Are you planning to apply for a place at university? 'Going to university' is something which over 300,000 people do each year, committing several years of their lives and a fair amount of money in the process. If you are planning to join them, this book is a guide through the increasingly complex maze of choices in higher education. It will show you how to get the best from the system, how to choose what is most appropriate, how to satisfy yourself about quality, how to decide where to live, how to get good advice about a career, and many other topics. Follow the expert advice in this book, and make sure you make the right choices at this important stage of your career. You may not get a second chance. Dr Dennis Farrington has worked in senior positions in university administration since 1981. He is a leading authority on the institution-student relationship and the way universities work.

160pp illus. 1 85703 405 8.

How To Books

How To Books provide practical help on a large range of topics. They are available through all good bookshops or can be ordered direct from the distributors. Just tick the titles you want and complete the form on the following page.